A Kingdom of Surprises

A
KINGDOM OF
SURPRISES

Cecil E. Sherman

BROADMAN PRESS
Nashville, Tennessee

© 1985 ● Broadman Press
    4215-33
ISBN: 0-8054-1533-5
Dewey Decimal Classification: 226.4
Subject Headings: THE BIBLE. N.T. LUKE / / JESUS CHRIST-
PARABLES
Library of Congress Catalog Number: 85-4699
Printed in the United States of America

Library of Congress Cataloging in Publication Data

Sherman, Cecil E.
  A kingdom of surprises.

  1. Bible. N. T. Luke—Criticism, interpretation, etc.
2. Jesus Christ—Parables. I. Title.
BS2595.2.S5   1985   226'.406   85-4699
ISBN 0-8054-1533-5

In appreciation to
the congregation of
First Baptist Church,
Asheville, North Carolina,
a listening people.

Contents

Introduction

Ronald Reagan opts for unilateral disarmament. Now that's a surprise! Bella Abzug marries a seminary student and becomes a submissive housewife. I don't believe it! Ralph Nader is asked to be president of a Baptist college. No way! The Dallas Cowboys fire Tom Landry. It didn't happen! The Chicago Cubs win the World Series. Hasn't happened in the memory of middle-aged men! Jerry Falwell dismantles the Moral Majority and joins the American Civil Liberties Union. Tell me it didn't happen! Andrei Gromyko defects to the West declaring he was really on our side all along. Couldn't be!

If any of the above had a shred of truth, all of us would be surprised. All of us have a pretty good idea who those people and organizations are. Since we know them, we have a mental picture of what they will do and can do. Further, we have found those people predictable. This means we know what they stand for and what they stand against.

What do you know about Jesus Christ? Probably you see Him as encased in the most predictable organization on the face of the earth—the church. What He said has been known for centuries; He is devoid of surprises. His words and ways have been analyzed, examined, pored over, and pondered. To package Jesus as a surprise would take some doing.

What I have just written is "conventional wisdom." Let's push on that assumption (that we know all about Jesus). If we do know all about Jesus, then why do we keep on writing new commentaries? Has it not all been said? The reason each generation writes those new commentaries and shelf after shelf of books about Him and His words is plainly and simply this: we do not know all about Him. The words of Jesus are like a mine deep within the earth. Fathers go in and dig in the mine and find coal that keeps them warm in the winter and turns on the lights in the dark. So the sons take up where the fathers left off. They go into the mine and dig. And the cycle does not appear to be slowing. The children after us will go into that mine too. They are finding the necessaries for life. And the mine shows no sign of running out of coal.

If you are of a literal bent of mind, you may find your surprises in Jesus when you see the miraculous. He fed a multitude with five loaves and two fishes. That is amazing! He made lame people to get up and walk; surely that is astounding. He patiently endured His cross and the resurrection still brings a sense of awe. I believe every word. But the miracles are far beyond me until I draw back from any notion that I could attain to or imitate such a supernatural being. Actually, I unconsciously mark down the miracle. Jesus is so different from me until He no longer seems a model. I say, "I couldn't do that. He is divine. I am not." And that is that. Millions of people think just that way about Him.

But also in the gospel story is a series of stories. These are called parables. All the Gospels carry them, but Luke seemed to have a special gift for passing along to us the stories of Jesus. In these stories we get inside the mind of Christ. We have windows into His head, glimpses of the way God looks at things. What is foolish, what is wise? What is earthbound, and what is of heaven? What is godly, and what is of the flesh? These questions are rarely answered point blank. More often Jesus would tell a story; the story gave His answer to the question.

I am a child of the church. From my earliest days I have been in church, in a church college, and in a seminary. I know the conventional wisdom church dispenses. I have been shaped by and helped by that wisdom. Now I work for a congregation as pastor. One of my first tasks is to persuade people to be a part of the life of the church. I am inside, not outside the church.

But careful study of the parables brings some surprises. Jesus is not trapped in that stained glass window. He is who He is. His words speak, fairly scream at us. When we are more American than kingdom of God, He has a word for us. When we are more establishment than kingdom of God, He has a judgment for us. When we are more safe than chance, He has an example for us. When we are more Pharisaic than open, He has a word for us.

None of us knows it all. I am dependent on the scholarship and the pastoral insights of all the generations of Christians who have gone into the mine of the parables and dug for meaning. They have helped me. Some of what I have to say will hardly be unique, strange, far-out. Maybe I will just say it in a way where you can understand. God uses personality keys to unlock our minds. My gifts do not unlock all minds. But the key I am does fit for some. I bring insight to them, and that is my reason for being.

All of these sermons were given while I was pastor of The First Baptist Church of Asheville, North Carolina. They are a most wonderful congregation. They forgave much of me. Out of pastoring them I was sent into the mine to bring forth warmth and light. Perhaps some of these sermons will do as much for you. They are offered with that prayer.

1
A Parable of Encouragement

Luke 8:4-15

Built into my childhood was a happy accident. I was born in town, went to school and church in town, had a town address. But just to say that I was reared in the city does not tell the truth. Nine miles from our home was my grandfather's farm. At least once a week our family would make the trip to the farm. The farm was not imposing; it was only fifty acres. About twenty acres were given to pasture, and the thirty remaining were under cultivation. To go there was exciting, it was like stepping into the nineteenth century. The plows were pulled by mules. The water came from a well. Bacon came from the smokehouse. The eggs were gathered each day. Cows had to be milked, pigs slopped, and mules fed. I remember the farm as a busy, lively, even exciting place.

But more than the excitement of the farm was the spirit of the farmer. This farm was in north central Texas, just nine miles from Fort Worth. There was no irrigation. My boyhood years spanned the years of the Dust Bowl and the Great Depression. Prices for produce were low; people were broke. Worst of all, there was the drought. Rain just would not come.

I was but a boy, but I remember clearly the conversations about drought. I did not understand all that was being said, but I caught the spirit of desperation. My grandmother worried, fretted. My grandfather was of a different spirit. Each day he would rise before sunrise, do milking chores, and eat a hearty breakfast. With genuine optimism he would set out to do the things a farmer had to do. He did not worry about the rain. It was not in his control. But to the fullest he did what he could do to have a good farm. My wise grandfather recognized that all of the harvest was not in his hands. He could only do so much.

When Jesus was among us He taught His disciples, then sent them out to preach the coming of the kingdom of God. Those first disciples carried good news. To the anxious, there came a gospel of peace. To the guilty, there was offered a gospel that was food for the soul. To the earthbound, there was offered a gospel that was eternal life. If you think about it, there could not have been a more hopeful offer. Looks like everyone would have hurried to become disciples. But it did not happen that way.

In spite of the beauty and the hope—the truth and the integrity of the gospel—what really happened is that a few people believed, but most people did not. Why? What went wrong? Is the gospel unable to save? Or, did we not deliver the gospel in the right way? By the time the New Testament was written, it had become apparent that most Jews were not going to recognize Jesus as Messiah. In fact, they were plainly opposed to Him. How could this be? What did it mean?

Jesus anticipated our need. He spoke a parable for our encouragement. Too often this parable has been dissected, pulled apart, analyzed as if it were a frog in a biology lab. Preachers just like me talk about stony ground and hard paths, but Jesus was trying to tell us more. I believe he wanted to speak a parable of encouragement. Jesus made us idealists in the first place; surely He wants to sustain us in the tasks He gave us to do.

The Capacity to "Take in" the Gospel Is Subjective, not Objective.

Jesus was a transparent man—a teacher whose words were in complete harmony with who He was and what He did. But midway through His ministry Jesus consciously went to a method of teaching we know as parables. He did this because so many people *were not understanding* Him. He was not reaching them one way; he would try another. Alfred Edersheim said all parables had one thing in common: "They are all occasioned by some unreceptiveness on the part of the hearers".[1] This would mean previous methods had brought little fruit. How could the clearest of teachers be misunderstood? Let me offer this explanation, and you decide if it is a faithful interpretation of the text.

The hearers of Jesus had divided themselves into two groups:

One group believed. They were open to all He said; they listened with spongelike minds. They wanted to hear, to understand.

But right beside them and often right in front of Jesus as He spoke was another group of people. These people wished Him ill. They were His die-hard opposition. They hoped He would stumble. They tried to entrap Him as He taught.

Now let's imagine Jesus as He spoke a parable. One part of his crowd was open, believing. The other part was hostile; they truly believed His teachings and His miracles were works of the devil. Would a parable help the hostile part of His crowd to understand? No. They have already made up their minds about Him. Anything He said would only be twisted to confirm their low opinion of Him. Such people are like the child's verse about prejudging:

> I do not like thee, Dr. Fell,
> How or why I cannot tell;
> Only this I know full well,
> I do not like thee, Dr. Fell.

An illustration some parents can understand might go like this: your daughter is a senior in high school. She is asked out by a boy who attracts her but disturbs you. You try to explain to your daughter why she should not go out with this boy. Surely you know how your daughter is going to react to what you say. She is going to reject out of hand what you have to say. This does not mean you have not arranged your arguments well. It does not mean that if you had used an illustration from your youth, she would have heard you. She is predisposed not to hear you. A parable, an illustration from your own experience—nothing will do.

Now let's bring this idea back to the gospel. As the seed is sowed, some will surely fall upon a kind of soil that is unresponsive. This does not mean the sower or the seed is at fault. It is the quality of the soil that determines the effectiveness of the seed. So some interpreters have called this teaching "the parable of the soils." The capacity to "take in" the gospel is subjective more than it is objective.

The Assignment Is to Sow the Good Seed; the Size of the Harvest Is Beyond Us

Gospel rejection is hard for us. In all sorts of ways we have tried to explain why people reject the gospel. What makes people turn away from Christ? To a person who has accepted Him, it is unexplainable. Sometimes we have become irrational in the face of entrenched, yielding unbelief. As Jesus was on His way to Jerusalem for His crucifixion, he passed through a Samaritan village. His disciples went before Him to tell the people He was coming. "But the people there would not receive him" (Luke 9:53). At this rejection, two disciples, James and John, lost their composure. They said to Jesus, "Lord, do you want us to call fire down from heaven to destroy them?" (Luke 9:54). Jesus would have none of such harsh measures. But from the beginning, disciples have not known what to do with folks who reject Jesus.

Built into us there seems to be a quest for a sure thing. We want to use gospel seed that is 100 percent guaranteed. We want that "money back guarantee." All the seed we sow has to come up, mature, and bear fruit in fullest measure.

Some of the people who are most zealous about evangelism are most ingenious in devising ways to make for a certain harvest. These people go to elaborate ends to see to it there will be a harvest when they preach. None of this contrived, arranged, managed evangelism is in the New Testament. Our assignment is not to arrange the harvest. Our job is to sow the good seed. But since the ways of American business have been brought into

the life of the church, it is understandable that we want to
guarantee that the church will grow. It must grow. If it does not
grow we ought to get a new president, coach, or pastor. Certainly both pastors and their people are at fault if the gospel seed
is not being put to the soil. But the harvest is not in our hands.

This parable has within it a powerful teaching often over-
looked. We are the people who sow the good seed of the gospel.
Jesus Christ Himself has given to us the work of sowing. Sometimes I do not want to sow the seed because of the mess and
confusion that come when others try to force a harvest. But this
is beside the point. If others have done a poor job, there is a
greater need for us to do a good job. In all the ways God gives
you, in all the places that are your life, you are the children of
those first disciples. The good seed of the gospel has been entrusted to us. Our assignment is to sow good seed; the size of
the harvest is not in our hands.

The Prospect for the Kingdom of God Is Strong;
Growth Will Surely Come

I have a bare spot under some elm trees in my front yard. The
past two summers I have been sowing some grass seed in those
bare spots. I take a rake and scrape the ground about a quarter
of an inch deep. Then I sow the grass seed into this broken
ground. For ten days to two weeks I keep the ground moist by
watering. At the beginning of last summer I went through this
process with some seed that was old. I got very limited results.
I put the old seed in the garbage can. It was no good. I went
to the hardware store and bought new, productive seed. Why do
such hard work if the seed is no good?

What is the parable of the sower or the parable of the soils
all about? I think the root teaching of the basic meaning is this:
Have confidence in the good seed of the gospel. It is going to
come up. Plant it. It will give harvest. Wait with patience.

There will be times when we know this with our heads and
even remind ourselves with our mouths that the seed is good—
that it will yield the harvest we desire. Still, we are human.
There will be times when we are faint of faith. But let's not take

our doubts too seriously. In these times it is helpful and encouraging to remember that some of the giants of faith also felt faint. People who saw and heard Jesus in the flesh were no more immune to doubts than we.

John the Baptizer identified Jesus and baptized Him. But when he was imprisoned by cruel Herod, John grew faint of heart. He sent two friends to Jesus asking, "Are you the one John said was going to come, or should we expect someone else?" (Luke 7:19). John had second thoughts. He was about to give up on Christ. When Peter stepped from the boat onto the water, at first he walked as did Jesus. Then he began to think about what he was doing. He doubted. What he was doing made no sense. And at that point he began to sink (see Matt. 14:28-30). He was giving up on Christ's power over the natural order. At the occasion of the death of Jesus, all of the disciples were scattered. Some went home and began to fish.

Some of us would rather go back to fishing. Some even long for Eden's innocence. Those who were more idealistic among us are tempted to idealism's opposite—cynicism. All great causes are tarnished. All sacrifice and self-giving is a hoax. All goodness is tinsel. Santa Claus is dead. And some wonder about God. Since we have discovered evil, it seems overwhelming. Will we, too, cut out?

I will not. I'm not going to buy into the defeatism and the opportunism that comes with such despair. God is not dead. Gospel seed has been sown all over the world. God knows where that seed is. There is life in that seed. This life will burst forth in God's good time. It's not the way we would have done it. We want immediate results. But God's kingdom is one of surprises. Where and when we least expect the seeds to burst forth with life, they will.

A number of years ago, some seed was taken from one of the pyramids in Egypt. It had been stored in a jar. For some five thousand years it had been quiet, still, dormant. Some archeologists found it and planted it. Then a strange thing happened. It germinated. It came up. It grew. What seemed to be dead still had life in it.

2
The Good Samaritan

Luke 10:25-37

An American couple were traveling across the lonely savannas of Africa. Their Land Rover broke down; they were stranded far from help. Some outlaws saw them, knew they had some food and money, so they fell upon them. These savage desperadoes took their food and money, and when the American man tried to protect his wife and his goods, they beat him. What was left was a sorry sight. The man was bleeding from several wounds; one leg was broken from the fight. His wife was trying to patch him up. She was without water, medicine, food, or transportation. The road was isolated. If the man did not get help soon, he could die.

A team of European agriculturalists were in East Africa examining the drought and famine. They were a happy lot, singing and telling jokes as they bounced over the rough back roads. All of a sudden they came upon the wounded, stranded American couple. Obviously there was great need, but also it was obvious that there was great danger. There was a brief, sharp argument about whether or not they should stop and offer aid. Rather than taking a risk they decided they would call from the next government station. So they sped away.

Some missionaries from the United States were on their way to Nairobi to attend a meeting. They were late; emergencies at home had made them start later than they had planned. If they were not present to make their report, their lonely, struggling little mission might not be funded next year. It was crucial that they stay on schedule. When they rounded the curve and came upon the broken-down American couple, all kinds of guilt came over them. If they stopped, they would miss their part in the meeting. If they did not stop, they would deny a part of the reason they were missionaries in the first place. With great shame the missionaries hurried on by.

An hour later some Russians came down the road. They were in Kenya to explore the possibility of entering into trade and cultural exchanges with the government. On an afternoon off they decided to drive through the back country. They came upon the American couple, saw they were in desperate circumstances, picked them up, and took them to a hospital. It was not easy. The American man was badly hurt and a mess. The woman was beginning to panic. But mess and panic and all, they delivered them to the hospital and told the administrators they would cover all expenses. Then they were gone.

The little story I just told you is fictional, but what I did to the categories in your mind was no more upsetting than what Jesus did with the perceptions of the people who first heard the story of the good Samaritan.

In Jesus' day there was a group of people whose job it was to interpret the Law. These people were scribes, but really they were ecclesiastical lawyers. Their job was to interpret the Jewish law. One of these lawyers asked Jesus the question that led to the Samaritan story.

The question was simple enough: "Teacher, what shall I do to inherit eternal life?" (Luke 10:25, RSV). Jesus threw the question back at the man. He asked him to quote the summary of the Law taken from Deuteronomy 6:5 and Leviticus 19:18. The man did, and that should have been the end of the matter. But the lawyer pushed Jesus. He asked a second question: "And who is my neighbor?" (Luke 10:29, RSV). That question is still alive today as it was in the time of Jesus.

What if the lawyer's question were put this way: "Who are the people I am bound to bother with?"[1] Now we are into a totally different matter. This concerns food stamps and Social Security, foreign aid and church budgets, tithes and the United

Way. But Jesus wanted to explore all of these matters. That is why he told the disturbing and compelling story of the good Samaritan.

A Disconcerting Heterodoxy

One of the passions of Jewish lawyers was the desire to get everything in place. So they asked questions like: "How much can I do on the sabbath?" "Under what conditions may I pull my ox from the ditch on a sabbath?" "When are my hands ceremonially clean?" "Were the disciples of Jesus really threshing grain when they pulled some kernels of grain from the stalk on the sabbath day?" And, of course, the big question was the one Jesus was asked several times in His ministry: "What must I do to gain eternal life?"

The Old Testament is a very specific book. The duties in sacrifice were spelled out in minute detail. If thus and so happens, that is a sin. Now here is what you do if you get in such a predicament. You take so much grain and wine, and you go before the priest. He will tell you exactly what to do. Make that sacrifice, and your sins will be covered. Everything was laid out. Nothing was left to doubt or to chance. There was a right way, and there were many wrong ways. Do it right. So the Jewish lawyer's question about the neighbor was an extension of an Old Testament idea: let's define this thing once and for all. Let's get it down right. The man wanted "his moral duties to be labelled and defined with the Talmudic precision to which ceremonial duties had been reduced."[2]

Seven hundred years ago Thomas Aquinas wrote a systematic theology in several volumes. In those volumes Thomas lined out the sum of theology. It was a complete statement. Many Christians thought the writings of Thomas were the final word. Out of this point of view came what we call *scholasticism*. Scholasticism did not approach education with an inquiring mind. The scholastic knew all truth. His job was not to inquire or explore. He was only to pass on that which he was fully confident was the sum of the truth.

We are latter-day scholastics. We know the sum of the truth. We have all the answers. And if we do not have all the answers, we are ready to follow the people who tell us they have all the answers. We set our categories just as tightly as did the Jews. The Russians are bad guys. They must be kept in that light.

Jesus took many categories of the Jewish world and threw them out the window and made up a story. In that story He took the most hated of people, the Samaritans, and made one of them the hero of the story. This is a classic case of not drawing within the lines. He took the good people, the priests and the Levites, and made of them bad people. Let's don't miss how stark Jesus' story was.

The compassionate man did not come from Jerusalem; he came from Gerizim. Gerizim was the place where false worship was practiced. The man was not of the right religion. He was a worshiper of the pigeon. Samaritans had defiled the Temple with human bones. The testimony of a Samaritan would not be admitted in a Jewish court. No self-respecting Jew would sit down to eat with this man. But in spite of his heresy and ignorance, he performed better than the orthodox priest and Levite.[3]

There is much to be said for thinking right. And to the extent that we are able, the Bible instructs us to straighten our warped minds, unravel our twisted theology. But tied to straight thinking about God there is the companion theme of doing right by our fellows. Straight thinking and right actions are not at cross-purposes except when poor religion confuses them. Orthodoxy apart from compassion is an offense to God. Anytime your categories of friends and enemies becomes so firm until you can use your theology to justify ignoring human need, you can be sure you have ceased to be a disciple of Jesus.

It was Jesus who made the Samaritan a hero in His story. It was Jesus who commended the extravagance of the woman who broke the perfume over Him. It was Jesus who took His disciples from the wrong parts of Jewish society. It was Jesus who went to the homes of the publicans and sinners. Right theology about God does not limit the obligation to associate, to touch, to be a part of.

Extravagant Compassion

If we decide that we have some obligation for all of the human family, then how much are we beholden to do for them? As Walter Russell Bowie put it: "What do you *have* to do in order to be respectable?"[4]

Recall what the good Samaritan did for the wounded Jew. He stopped when others would not, did not. He stopped at considerable risk to himself. He gave the robbers a clear shot at him.

He ministered to the man. When he "bound up his wounds, pouring on oil and wine" on them, that was all the medicine of that day could offer.

He put the man upon his "beast" and took him to a safe place. He could have concluded that he had finished his mission of mercy when he left the man after giving first aid.

He promised the innkeeper money for such time and food as the wounded man might need to get well. It was not just a casual act of mercy. It was a long-term, see-it-through sort of commitment.

There isn't a hint in the story of judgment upon the wounded man for getting in his predicament in the first place. Everyone knew that the road from Jerusalem to Jericho was dangerous. That's why Jesus used that road as a part of His story. Robbers hid in caves and in rocks. Even the Romans could not make that road completely safe for travel.

Now if there is such popular knowledge that this road is dangerous, might we not leave the wounded man on the ground and hurry on to our appointments with a rationale like this: the man knew this was a dangerous road. If he had used the good sense God gave him, he would not have been here in the first place. Or, since this is a dangerous road, the man should have been traveling in the company of others, so he would not have exposed himself to such risk. It is his own fault that he is in this mess. None of this muddy thinking clutters the story.

Why would I take your minds down such a slippery path? To what purpose would I even ask you to think so? Let me turn the question in on us. When the time comes for us to show continuing, long-term charity and compassion, do we not begin to think of all the things this poor man might have done to escape this condition? If we can make the man's predicament something of his own doing, then we are excused from charity. So in our own time, why are the poor as they are? Is it not their own fault? Are they not lazy? If they are lazy, then we are not obligated to care for them. Or, is there not some way we can help only the "worthy poor?" Then we become detectives trying to sort out the "worthy poor."

From time to time we read reports of people who have been cheating on welfare. For a certain kind of mind, the presence of any cheating only makes the more difficult and the more offensive the presence of welfare at all. To tell the truth, some of us don't have the capacity to be compassionate in an extravagant way. If such is your state, pray that God will amend your spirit until you have the Samaritan's capacity for extravagant compassion.

If God did not have extravagant compassion upon us in our sins, none of us would have access to His presence. Only an extravagant grace has made us His children. Let's get things in perspective. From God's point of view one sinner may be just about as bad as another. God may not be able to see much difference in my smug, self-sufficiency and the welfare cheaters grasping for more food stamps. Both are wrong. But is it not more becoming for us to face our own sins and enlarge our own capacity for compassion?

Inclusive Fellowship

At the end of the story Jesus asked a question of the ecclesiastical lawyer: "Which of these three, do you think, proved neighbor to the man who fell among the robbers?" (Luke 10:36, RSV). The reply of the lawyer is very revealing. The obvious answer to the question was simply, "The Samaritan." But the

Jewish lawyer could not get Samaritan to come from between his teeth. He could not say the word. Rather, he hid from the full truth by saying, "The one who showed mercy on him" (Luke 10:37, RSV). Martin Luther made acid comment on this reply. Luther said, "He will not name the Samaritan by name, the haughty hypocrite."[5]

But I am more like that Jewish lawyer than I want to admit. So fast and so firm, so hard and so petrified are some of my categories until I will not admit good of them either. In these days I am locked in a struggle with some other Christians. These people are my opponents. Since they are my opponents in a theological war, I must defeat them, say hard things about them, turn away from any good they may do. I would make of them Samaritans. I may come to the point that I cannot see good in them. I am the Jewish lawyer all over again.

The difficult truth and the first truth in the story of the good Samaritan is that all people are our neighbors. I do not want to hear this. It is too hard. It does not meet my previously agreed-upon categories of good guys and bad guys. But the parable bites. Jesus does not say what He is supposed to say. He says what He says. He makes us open a shut case. Samaritans are *bad*. Now we are in a bind. Since the story of the *good* Samaritan, there must have been at least one good Samaritan, and that opens the door to the possibility that there may be more. If there are more, then there are exceptions in the rules. If there are exceptions in the rules, then we may have to deal with each case on its merits.

Now we are getting down to the nut of the matter. God deals with each case on its merits. All of our fixed theology is but a shadow of a larger truth we dimly see. Only in Christ is the Word made flesh. For an instant in time God drew back the curtains and let us see in flesh a clear picture of the way He thinks, the way He works, and the way He measures the human family. We cannot build a theology from a parable, a short story of a few verses. But we get a clue into the mind of God. He's looking for extravagant mercy and compassion from His children. This extravagant compassion is not to be restricted to just a part of the human family. By creation God is the Father of us all. This means that all people are our family. Every person is my brother or sister.

Locked in that last question of Jesus is a word that bores in on us. Jesus asked, "Which of these three, do you think, *proved* neighbor?" (Luke 10:36, RSV). If we are to be the disciples of Christ, we are going to have to rise above our roots, our heritage, our state boundaries. We are going to have be neighbors to a larger part of the human family than yet we have been.

Perhaps there is a part of the modern psyche that is peculiarly offended by this story. We live in a time that has been called the "me" generation. Sometimes we speak of ourselves as being given over to "self-gratification." Self-gratification and the whole idea of the good Samaritan are going in opposite directions. Which way are we going?

3
The Rich Fool

Luke 12:13-21

How do you decide who the smart folks are? Be careful. The answer you give may tell me more about you than you want me to know. Who are the smart folks?

You have heard the expression: "Where is the smart money?" This means there is a kind of person who has studied, calculated, examined. This smart person has invested himself in ways that are calculated to pay off. He reads sporting journals. From time to time they offer tips on how to bet money on professional football. Teams that play three road games are likely to lose against the spread on the third road game in a row. Such is the world of smart money in professional sport.

Wall Street has its smart money people. These are the people who can anticipate trends in business or in consumer taste. With this sense of anticipation, these smart people can invest where demand is going to be. They get the jump on the average investor. So before demand drives prices up, smart money has already bought. They have at a lower price what the average investor will buy at the inflated price.

What in the world am I talking about? Why we would be on such a subject at all? What has smart money to do with Jesus and the Christian life? It seems to me that the Bible is so far out of sync with the average American that we cannot hear what Jesus said; we cannot understand the Bible. Put bluntly, I think most of us would not fault the rich fool. We would think him to be smart. For the record, here is exactly what he did:

1. He made his money in an innocent way; he earned it honestly.
2. He must have been hardworking, for his land brought forth "plentifully" (Luke 12:16, RSV). Hard work is a virtue.
3. He invested and expanded. "I will . . . build larger" (Luke 12:18, RSV).
4. He made provision for his future. "You have ample goods laid up for many years" (Luke 12:19, RSV).

Now the question that comes front and center is this: Was that man smart? I suspect that if this story were taken out of the Bible, if the story could be divorced from Jesus, if the story were removed from the judgment that is attached to it—most of us would think this man smart. And sometimes when I take a careful look at the way I spend my time, energy, and my money, maybe I function as if that man were smart, too. I am not much different from you.

But the story *is* in the Bible. The story *does* fall from the lips of Jesus. The story *does* have judgment attached. So let us look very carefully at what God called a fool. If this man is a fool, then a lot of Americans are fools. If this man is a fool, then too many of us are not smart. For the popular notion of smart money is brought into question by the values of this story.

The Way a Fool Thinks

A fool always wants more. "The land of a rich man brought forth plentifully; and he thought to himself, 'What shall I do, for I have nowhere to store my crops?' And he said, 'I will do this: I will pull down my barns, and build larger ones; and there I will store all my grain and my goods' " (Luke 12:16-18, RSV). The first thought, the dominant thought, the ordering thought of the rich fool was for *more*.

Numerous are the stories about the very human desire to gather more. It seems no matter how much we have, we want more. The story is told about John D. Rockefeller, Sr., a man who possessed millions, maybe even billions. A reporter asked Mr. Rockefeller how much money he wanted to control, possess. The reply came quickly, "Just a little more than I am now making."

A large landowner in Puritan New England was chided for owning so much land. How much do you intend to buy? His answer was starkly simple: "Just the land that adjoins mine."

Tolstoi put the same idea into parable form. A Russian peasant was told he could have all the land he could walk around in the time between sunup and sundown. With the rising of the sun the peasant began his quick step around the land. In midmorning it seemed that he was moving too slowly. He increased his pace. There was no time for food at noon. As the noontime heat beat down upon him he hurried his pace even more. He must circle more and more land. In midafternoon he was wet with sweat. He was tired. He had walked around a huge section, but still he burned for more. He began to run. Breathlessly he pushed himself into a fatigue he had never known. His heart beat wildly. Sundown was at hand. As he raced toward the point of beginning, a point that would make him the largest landholder in the district, he fell to the ground dead. And what drove Tolstoi's peasant to kill himself? The desire for *more*. But all of us fools think *more* is the smart way to go.

Jesus said: "Take heed, . . . a man's life does not consist in the abundance of his possessions" (Luke 12:15, RSV). And Goodspeed translates that verse this way: "It does not follow, because a man has abundance, that his life consists in wealth." And still a third way translators have worked with this verse is this: "For not in any man's abundance is his life (derived) from his possessions."[1] Are you always being smart when you opt for more? More may kill you. More may separate you from your children. More may drive a wedge between you and your wife. More may keep you from God's service and tie you simply to the gathering of things.

A fool wants a life of ease. Upon gathering many things, the response of the fool was, "I will say to my soul, Soul, . . . take your ease, eat, drink, be merry" (Luke 12:19, RSV). I suspect that ease was pretty important to the rich fool. I do not say this because I think the man had been lazy. In fact, the evidence is to the contrary. The man had been pushing so hard for so long that the prospect of ease was attractive indeed. The man could honestly say, "I have worked for years. I have taken little time away from my duties. The time has come when I deserve a break."

I am not an astute observer of the idle rich. My life has not put me in contact with these people that much. But such observation as I have had of these people, the "take your ease, eat, drink, be merry" people, these people are not very attractive. Much fine food, many fine clothes, the soft life . . . it seems to me these people become oblivious to the things of the spirit. Sensitivities wither. They cannot be concerned for others while they spend an inordinate amount of time caring for their own desires. The want of the poor is put out of their minds. Poor people are troubling. How can you "take your ease" while you worry about the plight of the poor. Retreat to some faraway place. Set distance between you and the needy of the world. This is the only way you can take your ease.

But where is Jesus? He is among the poor. He is with the sick. He is wrestling with great issues and great causes. Who is smart? If the idle rich are smart, then Jesus is not. If Jesus is smart, then the idle rich are not so smart in all their ease. Comfortable idleness is not a state commended by the Bible. And while many of us can dismiss this state as beyond our grasp, the sin of it all is that comfortable idleness is what we want whether we can get it or not. This is the state of mind of the fool.

A fool tries to nail down security. When you have used your IRA's to maximum advantage, when you have come to the time when you can pull out of Social Security all you have put in, when paid-up insurance becomes an annuity, when investments are called in—here is what you are supposed to say: "Soul, you have ample goods laid up for many years" (Luke 12:19, RSV). This is security.

This is only an opinion, but it seems to me that security is more tempting to Americans today than great wealth. If I read the times right, I think more smart money is put on security than on the gamble for more. We are not so venturesome as we were. We are more inclined toward security than once we were.

Where we are in life has something to do with how we hear this part of the parable. When we are young, we may disdain any word about security. We may gamble our way through our careers. Taking chances is not hard for us. Any word about security goes against the grain. But when we get a little older, we see that some gambles need to be covered, some bets need to be hedged, some risks need to be insured. Then we begin to take a more conservative approach. By the time old age comes upon us, we have become much different from what once we were. In advanced years we hope we have enough money to cover our last illness. We hope we do not outlive our wealth. We save, skimp, pinch pennies. Strange is the notion but strange and true: in those pennies is our security.

At church on Sunday we know better than we do. We may have some guilt about such misplaced trust. But security is the false god all old people have to fight off. A fool thinks he can make security with the gathering of things. Or is that fellow really smart? Who are the fools? Who are the smart folks? How people answer may tell us more about them than whether they have been through our baptisteries. Where is our security? Some think in greater armaments and national strength. Some think in land and wealth. Jesus gives another word. God takes care of His own.

The Things a Fool Never Thinks About

A fool never thinks carefully about ownership. Throughout the story the rich fool is under one big illusion: He assumed he owned, controlled, possessed. The barns were in his hands. He would put them up, or he would pull them down. The crops were his by right. He had grown them. He had harvested them. They were his to do with as he pleased. There was the beguiling sense of permanence about the present condition. What was his, was his. It had always been his. It would always be his.

The Bible doesn't buy this point of view. In fact, the Bible says that is not the way things are. "But God said to him, 'Fool! This night your soul is required of you; and the things you have prepared, whose will they be?' " (Luke 12:20, RSV). The rich man really did not control, possess, the things he thought he did. Jesus taught another point of view on possessions. They are temporary. They are fleeting. They are ephemeral, transient. "Do not lay up for yourselves treasures on earth, where moth and rust consume and where thieves break in and steal" (Matt. 6:19, RSV). Then Jesus pursued this line of reasoning: "But lay up for yourselves treasures in heaven, where neither moth nor rust consumes and where thieves do not break in and steal" (Matt. 6:20, RSV).

There are two kinds of investments:

(1) You can invest in things that last until you die, but if you make this kind of investment you will have to spend much time and care, for such stuff can so easily be taken by the thief or lost in the stock market or eroded by a changing world.

(2) You can invest in heavenly acts of kindness. You help the child. You can invest in the future of a school that does God's good work. You can send the missionary with God's good news. It is a different kind of an investment.

Hearing—really hearing Jesus will change your priorities. Understanding Him will change the idea of where the smart money is being invested. Instead of having our wealth tied up in securities and stocks and lands and bonds, we will invest in the future of truth, mercy, hope, and heaven.

A fool never thinks about giving anything away. Ideas like stewardship, responsibility, social obligation are missing from this parable. The man never saw beyond himself. And this kind of thinking is on the increase among us. Consider the following:

- How many Americans are dropping out of the mainstream, and are getting into the underground economy? They pay no tax. They keep no books. They are not accountable to anyone. It is a private world where me and mine are the sum of all that is.

- Too many Americans are no longer willing to bear their part of the citizenship that is the duty of us all. They will not vote. They will not register for the draft. They will not vote taxes upon themselves. They have little heart for the poor or their problems. "Let the poor fend for themselves" is their attitude.

- And let us not excuse ourselves. Too many people in our churches are content for someone else to bear the burden of churchmanship. We make money. The idea that we are beholden to give away money . . . such thought has not yet dawned upon us. So the burdens of our national life, our town life, and our church life are unevenly borne. This does not mean that the rain has not fallen on the "just and the unjust." God has given the rain to us all. God has given plenty to many. But some see no sense of obligation.

John Wesley, the father of Methodism, was great in his grasp of stewardship. His idea was that he should make all the money he could so that he could give away all the money he could.

> When he was at Oxford he had an income of £30 a year. He lived on £28 and gave £2 away. When his income increased to £60, £90 and 120 a year, he still lived on £28 and gave the balance away. The Accountant-General for Household Plate demanded a return from him. His reply was, "I have two silver tea spoons at London and two at Bristol. This is all the plate which I have at present; and I shall not buy any more, while so many around me want bread."[2]

Wesley was right. It is immoral for some of us to have two and three and four of the necessities of life while others have little or nothing. We are Christians. Our smart money ought be invested in heavenly things like the poor, the sick, the wartorn, and the helpless. If we would be rich toward God we must be smart in our investments. Have you thought about giving away some of your wealth. I do not mean that you ought give away your wealth for tax purposes. Give it away for health of your soul.

A fool never thinks about eternity. Stunning, stabbing is the word that comes from God in this parable: "Fool! This night your soul is required of you" (Luke 12:20, RSV). It was all over. The man was dead. His heart stopped beating. He was no longer in control of his lands, barns, and crops. He was through. All of his plans were put aside. There was no one to follow through on them. He was dead.

Charles II ruled England from 1660 to 1685. He was not a godly man. In the last years of his life he had a dream to build a palace at Winchester. It was to be a magnificent place. The last week of his life he gave orders that the house should have a lead roof. Within a week the king would have a lead coffin. And what of the palace? It stood half finished for years. It was used as a hospital for a time. It was used as a storage place or warehouse for a time. But when Charles II died, the dream was dead. It was all over.

Time is always with us. We are creatures of time. We cannot escape our time-bound condition. The fool forgot that he was not going to live forever. He made all of his plans for this world. In fact, we are citizens of two worlds. Two sets of books are kept on us:

- The one is kept by bankers, stock brokers, realtors, and lawyers. This is the stuff that we hold in this world.
- Another set of books is kept in heaven. Sometimes the book is called "the book of life" (see Rev. 22:19, KJV). Different things are thought valuable in God's books. What do you do with Jesus? Do you recognize Him as God's clearest Word to you? Do you see the goodness, the love, and the hope that He came to give all of us? Have you owned Him as Savior and Lord?

● Did you invest yourself in the kingdom of God? Did you give yourself to causes of mercy, of hope, and help? This counts with God. And what of the spread of His gospel? He favors those who go forth with the message. Have you entered into their work?

Jesus' way is not the popular way. To follow Him will make you strange. You will be out of step and out of sync. But the world and life and eternity must surely be like Jesus described it, else all spoken at church is a farce. Care. Think. Invest yourself and all that you hold the Jesus way. Be rich toward God (Luke 12:21).

4
The Rules for Our Accountability

Luke 12:35-48

Can you remember what it was like to be in high school? Back in the dark recesses of my mind, behind stacked file cabinets of more recent events, in a dusty corner hidden away—there is the place where I have all those high school memories stored. Make the journey with me. Try to remember.

High school was many things: fun in the halls and clowning around, memories of athletics, a few timid efforts at romance. But the last file folder in the drawer of high school memories concerns books, studies, and the classroom part of high school. My parents were kind of funny. They had this idea that the classroom part of high school was the most important part. They did not succeed in getting me to buy into that idea, but they did have a psychological victory. I had some guilt about not making my studies more important.

There was a reason for my casual attitude toward studies. In part, I was not a super student because I was lazy, immature, and distracted by other things. Still there was another reason: I did not have to study very hard to do well in high school. Most of the people around me were lazier than I was. Most of the kids were more immature than I was. Most of the kids were more distracted than I was. So I could make good grades and not work very hard. Deep down inside, I was hearing what my parents were saying. I knew the classroom side of high school was the most important part. And as I moved from sophomore to junior to senior years, my grades steadily improved. Some grading periods I would have all *A's*. Yet even as I made *A's*,

I knew I was not working hard at my studies, and buried in the back of my mind was an uneasiness: *What am I going to do when I get to college and have to work at the books?*

Finally, high school days ended. It was off to college. I was glad; I was sad. I wanted to leave home, but I really did love my family. Neither my mother nor father had gone to college. Both wanted their children to have the opportunity of college. I was the first, and I was off to Baylor. Baylor was a great place for me. The group was open and willing to take a green kid like me. For the most part the fun was clean. But Baylor was a little like my parents. They, too, had this funny idea about going to class and making good grades and studying hard.

As I went to college, I knew college was going to be different from high school. I knew the teachers were going to ask more of me, but I really did not know what to expect. How much reading is enough reading? How thorough is the research on a term paper to be? How much do you need to know to be prepared to take a final examination? And even more practical, where is a good place to study where the animals and clowns will let you alone?

I made a number of mistakes in my fumbling efforts to learn how to study and prepare for college work. It was an uncertain route. I made some bad grades at first, but with the passing of time I learned what was expected of me. I learned how to be a college student. Actually, I learned the rules for academic accountability. Until a student learns those rules, student life will be a hazardous occupation.

Now let's shift this same idea of accountability to another field. Micah, the prophet, asked the question of our accountability to God. "What doth the Lord require of thee?" (Mic. 6:8, KJV).

The Kingdom parables of Jesus are especially instructive in helping us deal with this question. With insights all at once profound and puzzling, Jesus sets out what God asks of us. Since most us who read books of this kind are of consciously or unconsciously trying to find out what God wants of us, perhaps these parables will answer some of our questions.

Like so many Kingdom parables, the basic part of the plot is this: God is pictured as the Master of a house, the Owner of a vineyard. He places His property in the charge of a servant. In the absence of the Owner, the servant has liberty to use and manage the Master's money, land, or house. And in all the parables, the Owner wants the servant to perform in a certain way until He returns. Now you have the basic plot. God is the Owner. We are the servants who are given trust, time, and freedom. What is expected of us in the brief interim when we are called on to manage the Owner's holdings?

We Are to Be Prepared for the Master's Return

How do you get ready for the return of the Master of all life, the Owner of all that is, the Keeper of time? It seems to me that people take two basic routes in making ready for His coming.

The first group makes ready with what I want to call *emergency behavior.* This may involve religious decision or commitment. I am not making light of such; in fact, at the end of our worship services I call on people to make religious decisions. For many it is the great need of their lives. In making ready for the coming again of the Master, some have gone on pilgrimage, set out on mission service, and given away fortunes. But all this is *emergency* behavior. It is a departure from the routine and the real and basic mission of your life.

A second way to make ready for the return of our Lord is simply to do well and faithfully the task that is ours to do. I think this is the sense of the teaching. In the stories of Jesus, the people who are doing their God-assigned task at the time of His coming are the people who were given the commendation of our Lord. And if you back off and think about it for just a little, this is the most hopeful interpretation of the parable. My daily life, my ordinary work, is blessed. It is what God wants of me. If I had to do some of the Herculean and heroic deeds of some of the saints to win our Lord's favor, I would be in trouble. I am neither a saint (in the popular sense), nor a hero. But the text tells me God will commend me if I do my daily work well. This is within my range. This I can do.

In addition to doing the tasks God has given us, He asks something more. *We are to live with sense of time.* The spirit of the parables is one of expectation and anticipation. Life is precious. Time is irreplaceable. We must be about our task. For when our summons comes, we want to be able to say, "It is finished." The work given us to do must be done and not left to another.

Here is a place where I see the pagan side of our culture. The Puritans often railed against frivolity. They were saying life was too important to be invested in foolishness. That is the sense of this parable. Life is important. We are about important work. To be doing nothing or doing the light or the careless . . . such is wasting time. Time is all we have and not much time at that. So I see the great ones concerned about the fast pace of time. John Keats worried aloud,

> When I have fears that I may cease to be
> Before my pen has glean'd my teeming
> brain,
> Before high piled books, in charactry,
> Hold like rich garners the full-ripen'd
> grain.[1]

The man was worried he would die before he finished the task that was his to do. In this, Keats was in step with the Gospels. Jesus would say, "I must work the works of him that sent me, while it is day: the night cometh, when no man can work" (John 9:4, KJV). How earnestly I pray I may be faithful to my task, and equally important, I pray I may finish the task assigned me. For in so doing I will be prepared.

We Are to Learn to Work Apart from our Master

Notice how often Jesus uses the same kind of a plot. The Master gives talents, then goes away. The servants are to use the talents *while the Master is absent* from them. He will come again and ask what they have done with what they were given (See Matt. 25:14-30). Similar in plot is the parable of the tenants in the vineyard. A Landowner planted a vineyard and prepared it thoroughly; then, the Landowner "rented the vineyard to tenants and *left home on a trip*" (Matt. 21:33-44). And in this parable the Master is *gone away for a time.*

Here is an idea that is relatively new to me. Of late I have been reading and thinking about the silences of God and absences of God. I have listened to and thought about certain of the Psalms that struggled with the apparent absence of God. This idea is hard for me to take in. I have been reared on preaching and a theology that has God near, available, immediate. I have always thought God was as near as a prayer. Scripture supports this kind of thinking. The early church appeared to live in the constant presence of God. The Spirit was guiding, lifting, encouraging. So we have come to think of the God who is near. We reach for the supporting text that tells us: "I will be with you always, to the end of the age" (Matt. 28:20).

But alongside these texts are others. The parables tell of a God who sets us on our way, steps back, and leaves us to do the work assigned, then returns and calls us to account. These parables seem to suggest that at least parts of our lives "will be lived without a conscious experience of God's nearness"[2]

So H. J. Cadbury would interpret this parable to say,

Much clearer from these parables comes the notion of an absentee God. Like the apocalyptic term *parousia,* they remind us that normally we are on our own and alone. For long intervals we have no contact with the one to whom we are responsible. He is in a distant country and there is no certainty that he will return soon. Our business is to live as we should live, but without him. Normal rectitude, fidelity, diligence, are expected of us.[3]

Why do I even bother you with such? This is a disturbing thought. But let's try to tell the truth. We are divided. Some among us declare we live out each day in the presence of God. He is near. But there is a different testimony that comes from the rest of us. We would like to say we experience God as a part of every day, but it will not come out. We cannot say it because it is not our experience. We come to church to find Him. But at church we are often made to feel guilty, a second-class Christian. We don't experience God as our constant companion.

This teaching ought to be some comfort. Maybe you are not so abnormal, inferior, or abandoned. It could be that you are doing what is expected. You are living out your assignment; you are doing your job as a stewardship to the Master who is coming. You are faithful to your work. You live in hope. I want to encourage you. Keep the faith.

All of us have some part of the child still alive within us. As a boy I was sometimes irresponsible. My mother would give me a job to do. As long as she stayed with me, looked over my shoulder, I was a hard worker. But if mother should give me a job to do and go away, I would slow down. Sometimes I would not work at all until I saw her coming.

Is not this the teaching of the parable? We are children in our stewardship. If we think we are going to be called to account soon, we get active. We clean up our lives, make a rededication, and get straight. But if the time of accountability does not seem near, we forget and grow careless. So if the doctor told me I was soon to die of a dreadful disease, I would get to work in all things spiritual. But since I seem to be enjoying good health and the time of accountability seems to be distant, I grow careless. The teaching of the parable is that we are to grow up—to be responsible stewards for God even when our accountability is not immediate.

We Are Graded on the Principle of Proportionate Opportunity

The last rule for our accountability I find in the text is about what God calls fair. On the surface it would appear that if God treated all of us the same, God would be fair. But this is not the teaching in the text. To get some idea of what Jesus called fair, consider the stiff judgment He put upon two villages where often He taught.

> How terrible it will be for you, Chorazin! How terrible for you too, Bethsaida! If the miracles which were performed in you had been performed in Tyre and Sidon, the people there would have long ago sat down, put on sackcloth, and sprinkled ashes on themselves, to show that they had turned from their sins! *God will show more mercy* on the Judgment Day to Tyre and Sidon than to you (Luke 10:13-14).

The key words are: "God will show more mercy" This means Tyre and Sidon are not going to be judged as are Chorazin and Bethsaida. The people of Tyre and Sidon are going to get more lenient judgment than the people of Chorazin and Bethsaida.

Jesus is stating a principle here. It is found throughout the New Testament. Our judgment will be on the basis of the spiritual opportunities we have been given. So if we have had a Christian home, religious education, and a chance to repent, believe, obey and serve, then we are doubly bound to take the opportunity. Now turn that idea over. People who have had but a small chance to know of God or are from a part of the world where the ways of God and His Christ are but faintly known will be judged gently. Since they have had but a small chance, they will be given gentle judgment.

Let's push this idea a step further. Often we think of judgment as being only on the basis of belief. So if we have believed in Christ, we will will be accepted of God. There is much Bible evidence for this point of view. But this isn't all. Also in the Bible are places that tell us we are to perform. Our belief must grow into acceptable, useful, merciful ministries in the kingdom of God. In the parable, the servant was to perform. In the Sermon on the Mount, the wise man was to build his house on the rock (see Matt. 7:24-27). In the last judgment Jesus described in Matthew 25:31-46, Jesus wanted service, compassion, and performance. We are to feed the hungry, clothe the naked, visit the imprisoned, heal the sick.

Who has had the very best chance to do what Jesus asked us to do? I cannot think of a more privileged generation than are we. We have enough to eat; in fact, more of us are struggling with gluttony than with starvation. We know the answers to some of the diseases that kill children in Africa. Our land produces more than enough for us. We store our extra cheese and grain. Our churches are rich. We have enough to share. We are the blessed. Not only do we have things and riches, we have a knowledge of God's expectation. The text lays a heavy word on us. "Much is required from the person to whom much is given; much more is required from the person to whom much more is given" (Luke 12:48). God is going to take account of our great opportunity when he calls us to judgment. These are sobering words. Since we have been given so much, we are going to be called to a stricter account. May we be found faithful. May God be merciful!

5
The Ways of God with the Chosen

Luke 13:6-9

When I was a boy, I lived next door to a family that was different from mine. They had a boy who was near to my age. This boy's name was Jimmy; we played together. But since our families were so different, our play was sometimes uneven. Jimmy did not have to do chores about the house and yard. In fact, it hardly seemed any of the family had work to do. They were careless about cleaning their house. The yard was not kept. I envied Jimmy. As soon as he got home from school Jimmy was ready to play. Usually I had to say, "I'll be out in a little while. I have some chores to do before I can play." I played part of the time, but I also had work to do. It was the way our family was ordered. Now that I am a little older, I suspect I was more fortunate than I recognized. Life is more than play. Somewhere, sometime all of us have to learn that something is expected of us. If it isn't, then life is without meaning. Jesus conveyed this same idea in a parable.

The stories of Jesus were clearer to the people who first heard them than they are to us. This is not because we are less intelligent. Rather, the reason for our difficulty in understanding lies in the setting. The parable in this chapter is about a fig tree and a gardener—about the proper time to wait for a fig tree to bear fruit and the economy of having trees around that do not produce. All of this sounds strange to us. It's beyond our experience.

How did Jesus' hearers understand the parable? Consider the following interpretation:

The fig tree is God's chosen people, Israel. *The Good News Bible* does not do justice to the language of the original. This tree had been chosen and given favored treatment beyond the other plants in the garden.

The expectation of fruit on this favored tree was an expectation that Israel would do God's work in the world. Nearly two thousand years earlier than Jesus, God had said to Abraham, "I will bless them that bless thee, and curse him that curseth thee: and in thee shall all families of the earth be blessed" (Gen. 12:3, KJV). Israel was jealous of her blessings. She was unwilling to pass them along to the "other families of the earth." Israel had not produced.

The gardener is the Messiah. And as in other places in the Bible, the Messiah seems to plead with the Owner of the garden —God. Note that the Messiah figure speaks mercy; the Owner asks productivity and presses judgment. Here we have the two faces of God.

Finally, there is the time frame that is the setting of life. Israel did not have all the time in the world to do the work assigned. The usual time given a fig tree to bear was three years. To have a tree that did not bear was bad. Good land was in short supply in that arid country. So all trees were watched. If they did not bear promptly, they were replaced.

Now you see how a story that is hard for us to understand would have been clear to the people who first heard it. All the extra meanings I have been able to explain were common knowledge to all when Jesus first spoke. Jesus was speaking judgment on the nation. To them He was speaking heresy. Out of His mouth in clearest language, in broad daylight, before God and everybody, Jesus was saying that God was going to do away with Israel and find another instrument to do His work in the world.

Did this happen? How did it happen? About forty years after Jesus spoke this parable, there came to Israel a judgment worse than the Babylonian captivity. The Romans came down upon them. The Temple was destroyed; it has never been rebuilt. And though in modern time there has come a new Israel, it is different from the nation Jesus spoke judgment upon. The tree was cut down. A basic witness of the church has ever been that she has taken up the work of the chosen. Now the church is about God's work in the world.

But if this be so, do we not put ourselves in the place of that favored tree in God's garden? Yes. We take to ourselves all the privileges and perils of the chosen. So this parable becomes threatening to us. We have been given a mission. We are expected to be productive. If the parable is to be more than historical interest, we will have to see that this parable spoken to us. We are the chosen, we are the fig tree, and we are the body from whom God expects good fruit. In this light, what does the parable say to us?

Expectation

Our text is but four verses. Is it not pressing the Scripture pretty hard to milk from it grand teachings, teachings that come from only four verses? That deserves some thought. My own view is: the idea of expectation is a theme found throughout the New Testament. I think this brief parable is supportive of a much larger body of Scripture which says about the same thing.

In Matt. 25:14-30, Jesus told a story about three servants. The master is about to leave home on a trip. He gives to one servant five thousand dollars; to a second servant he gives two thousand; and to the last servant he gives one thousand dollars. The master stays away for a time, but in due time he returns. The powerful teaching of the parable is the severe judgment pronounced upon the third servant. He was given only one thousand dollars, but he did not use what he was given. He hid the money in the ground and only gave back to the master what he was first given. The words Jesus put in the master's mouth are harsh: "You bad and lazy servant! . . . You should have deposited my money in the bank, and I would have received it all back with interest when I returned. Now take the money away from him and give it to the one who has ten thousand coins" (Matt. 25:26-28). The master's expectation of productivity is basic to the parable.

Jesus told another story about a faithful and an unfaithful servant. The master gives them both work to do. He goes away, but soon he returns. Upon his return he expected that his house would be in order, that the work would be well-done, that the servants had been faithful. (Luke 12:41-48). Though the circumstances of the story vary, the theme of Jesus' teaching is constant. The people who have been entrusted with special assignments from God are going to be measured. Something is expected of the chosen.

Other illustrations could be offered from the parables of Jesus, but this makes the point. That God expects something of His people is a constant, recurring teaching of Jesus.

Now that we know God is going to expect something of us, what does He expect? Here is what I think God expects of us:

God expects us to maintain our families. The family is a threatened institution in our society. The New Testament idea of family is what God wants; it is what He is going to be looking for when He measures us. Marriage promises are to be kept. Children are a trust from God. To help a child to a knowledge of God is a basic parental responsibility. God expects us to help in passing along our faith and passing along our values.

God expects us to be faithful in our vocation. In our work we are serving God. If you cannot serve God in your work, you need to get into some other work. Work is to be done as unto God. This means that poor work will rise up to be curse to us on the last day, for our work will be measured. Work that helps people, ministers to people, heals people—this kind of work is ministry whether our society chooses to call it ministry or not.

God expects us to be responsible citizens. The society we live in is an arrangement that is God-ordered. We need government. If we do not have good government, the weak will be abused, the clever will take advantage of the simple. Our laws are tools of justice and fairness. Our schools are instruments to help all the children. Our police are friends to the abused. Our courts are servants to justice. God expects us to work with government to make these noble ideas happen. Only good people can make good government. If government falls into the hands of bad people, then government becomes the oppressor of us all.

God expects us to be useful in His Kingdom work. Church is supposed to be about the work of the kingdom of God. To tell you to be about Kingdom work is to leave you unfocused. Church is to take you, aim you, and motivate you in God's service. So the church ought to send willing persons to the place of greatest need in doing the work of the kingdom of God.

When God lays an expectation upon us, He has not ruined us or diminished our lives. Look at a playboy. Is he useful, productive? Is he a blessing to the world? Does he risk himself for great causes? When does he deny himself for the sake of the poor or the oppressed? He does none of these commendable things. He is living up to no expectation. He is a taker, not a giver. God expects more of His chosen. This is why the church is ever risking herself when she functions like church. And when the church turns inward, gets lazy and self-centered, takes care of her baubles and extras rather than helping and witnessing, then the Church is in danger of falling under the judgment of this parable. We read it as a historical curiosity to our own peril. God works with His chosen in the same way today as He did two thousand years ago. He has laid an expectation upon us that is heavy and wonderful.

Grace

The Gardener in this parable is the Author of grace. It is He who pleads with the Owner. If we were careless we could conclude that God is really not one but at least two. One part of the Godhead argues for the removal of the tree. Another part of the Godhead asks mercy and grace. But before we slip into a heresy here, can we not remember the predicament of a parent? On the one hand the parent needs to provide discipline. Other times the parent sees the child's need for mercy and a second chance. If I can have both these ideas in my small head, surely God can do much more.

The Gardener asks for a second chance for the unproductive tree. "Leave it alone, sir, just one more year; I will dig around it and put in some fertilizer" (Luke 13:8). Here is the great word of the New Testament. God in Christ begs for all of us a second chance. Strange. Some are so unlearned in the ways of God until they think they have hardly had a first chance. But each of us had a first chance. We were told the ways of God. Each of us violated that first command. And each, in turn, has been put out of that first garden of innocence. But in Christ all of us are called back to the ways and the service of our Heavenly Father.

Look inside the New Testament. You see one after another the stories of a second chance.

● Peter denied Christ, but he had a second chance. He was forgiven and given a place of enlarged service.

● John Mark was with Paul on that first mission trip. He could not take it; he quit. But for John Mark there was a second chance.

● Paul was given all the privilege of Jewishness at its best. He misinterpreted his religious instruction. When he made the church his enemy and set out to persecute, Paul was calling good evil. But Paul was given a special visitation; he got a second chance.

The competitive world we live in is not especially forgiving. We get one chance. If we fail, we are out. With some pain I recall the story Barry and Margaret White told about their first child. She was bright and quick, but she did not work. The time came for her to take her college entrance exams. She was not prepared; she did poorly. In England, there is no second chance. For this potentially fine student, there was no second chance. For a lifetime in England that girl has been denied a college education. Happily, I did not live in a system so rigid. If I had, I could not hold the job I now have. For had I been required to be mature at the time I entered college, I would probably have failed. Grace, tolerance, time: these are the pieces Jesus brings to the life puzzles of us all. He buys for us a little more time. If I understand God's nature, it is not His desire to uproot us and replace us. I believe God wants us to become productive. And He gives us time.

Time

The urgency in the parable is lost on us. Let's see if we can find it. I have lived a part of my life in a country where water is precious. In West Texas water is not a joke; it is too scarce to joke about. Within this century there has come to West Texas a blight in the mesquite tree. It is a thorny tree that grows no larger than a dogwood. The tree is only useful as livestock feed. It will not make wood for burning, posts for fencing, nor boards for housing. The mesquite drinks up the water that is in the land.

So a whole industry has grown up around ridding the land of the mesquite tree. There are several ways to do it. Ranchers hire people to come to a pasture and get rid of the mesquite. You see, the mesquite is not innocent in its uselessness. Uselessness is immoral. If mesquite trees drink up all the water in the soil, the grass grows thin, and more rains do not fall—then the ranch goes broke. The home place is lost. One is out of business. So in the total economy of a producing ranch, a non-producing stand of mesquite trees can be the difference in making it and losing it. The rancher only has so many years to put up with the mesquite. If he doesn't get rid of them, they will get him.

Now let's move back to the parable. The economy of a garden in the Middle East is much like the economy of a ranch in West Texas. One only has so much water in the soil. One only has so much soil that will grow a good tree. One only has so much time before the stark reality of starvation closes in. So the Owner, recognizing the situation, is made to say, "Cut it down! Why should it go on using up the soil?" (Luke 13:7).

In our own time we seem to have divided people into three groups:

● There are *useful people*. These people work, help, produce.

● There are *innocent people who are useless.* They do not hurt anyone; they are living their lives at their own pleasure.

● And there are *harmful people.* We lock them up or try to control them. But we know they are hurting the common good.

No judgment is brought upon anyone in our society if one chooses to be *useful* or one of the *innocent useless.* Much that passes for the good life is really an appeal to join the *innocent useless.* I have read the Bible carefully. This three-shelf division of the human family is not found in the Bible. Useless and harmful become the same. So, the careless, frivolous, societal drop-out becomes immoral by biblical standards. This is a heavy word. We are the people who live for Friday afternoon, who long for vacation. Our real work is play. C. E. M. Joad spoke of us: "We have the powers of gods and we use them like irresponsible schoolboys."[1]

At this point I want to crawl around on the other side and speak a word for the useless. I do not think the useless intend to be useless forever. Sometime the useless intend to change and become useful. They see the present playtime in life as but a stage they will pass through.

But the parable is like a gathering of dark clouds that blight a pleasant day. "If the tree bears figs next year, so much the better; if not, then you will have it cut down" (Luke 13:9). Isn't this parable nearer life than the shallow thinking that passes for life? All of life is lived in a time frame. In a cemetery, we can see all sorts of messages on tombstones, but we can count on one thing: there will be a date of birth and a date of death. That means there was a time frame. The person buried under that stone had a limited amount of time to produce. Then, time ran out.

One may object by saying, "You are trying to scare us. Stop telling us death stories to move us to religion." I am not beholden to write only what pleases people. If deathbed stories go out of style, that means the styles have changed. I do have obligations. Is what I am saying true to the sense of the words of Jesus? Does this story suggest that all of life is lived within the urgency of time and time is precious and time is running out? I cannot be honest with the parable and leave that word unspoken.

What does this mean? It means we need to get about the work of God. Some need to confess Him. Already some believe, but to this point they have been quiet. Time is moving. Confess Him and move on to further work for Him. Some confessed Him as a child but are hiding from Him now. In their hearts they believe, but the truth is: they are about the business of making for a life for themselves. The work of God is on the back burner. They are being presumptuous. Time is running out. Now is the time to be about the work of producing for God.

I grew up in a blue-collar neighborhood. We had old cars we patched to keep moving, or we rode the bus. To take a taxi was out of the question. Such would be a luxury. I recall the first time I rode in a cab. The cabby pushed down the lever on his meter box. The meter began to tick. I was fascinated. But I was more than fascinated. Every few blocks the meter would jump. More and more, higher and higher went the number. I was unable to enjoy the sights of the new city for the meter that held me transfixed. Life is little bit like my first experience in a cab. My mission is to remind you: the meter is running. Time is moving. When are you going to produce for God?

6
The Humility Lesson

Luke 14:1; 7-11

Years ago I saw a cartoon in a magazine. Two ministers were walking in front of the church. The one must have said to the other, "Don't be holier than thou," for the caption beneath the cartoon had these words coming from an agitated minister: "But I am holier than thou!" What the cartoon said in fun is what all of us would say if we would only peel off the thin, cosmetic covering of manners that keeps all of us from saying all we think.

So when the solo is given to another member of the soprano section, several people are really thinking, *But I could sing that solo better than she.* When others are chosen for service on the board of deacons, real people in the congregation are thinking, *What made them choose that fellow? I am fully as qualified as he.* And every pastor who will tell the truth has often wondered to himself upon learning that a prestigious pulpit has been filled by Reverend Ordinary, *Why did they turn to that guy? I could have done the job better than he.*

The truth of the matter is that all of us spend a good bit of our time promoting ourselves. In sly fashion we go about this self-promotion. If we were head-on in our efforts our scheme would be recognized, and we would be discredited. The reason we do these things is because we have well-developed egos, high estimates of our abilities, and all of us have become skilled at explaining away our failures. We compare ourselves to people who are obviously human and flawed; this selective comparison makes us to look good while it makes the other fellow look bad.

Jesus met people like us. The Bible tells of an incident that speaks to our condition.

One sabbath, a day somewhat like our Sunday, Jesus was asked to go to the home of an important Pharisee. He did, and this ought to instruct us. Jesus did not just fuss with the Pharisees. He had a constant conversation with them. In all ways He knew them well, and that worked both ways. They came to know Him too. The invitation was to dinner. A sabbath dinner would not be casual; a strict etiquette would govern the style in which the meal was served and the ways the guests would act.

Ever observant, Jesus noticed the way the guests made their way into the dining room. The table arrangement would have been U-shaped. Guests would sit only on the outside of the tables. The center place at each of these three tables would be the place of honor. Jesus watched. Since the host was an important man, we may assume the most important people were invited to the home of this important man. They should have known the rules for polite social conduct. But what Jesus saw was crude, crass, and aggressive. As the guests came into the dining room, they hurried to grab the seats of honor. The people who came in later could take the lesser places.

Jesus may have reflected on what He had learned from Proverbs as a boy. We are reasonably certain this is true; listen to the Old Testament: "Put not forth thyself in the presence of the king, and stand not in the place of great men: For better it is that it be said unto thee, Come up hither; than that thou shouldest be put lower in the presence of the prince whom thine eyes have seen" (Prov. 25:6-7, KJV).

What was Jesus doing? Is this a lesson in social etiquette? Does this mean that you ought to be careful about the way you seat yourself when you go to a wedding rehearsal? Only in the most superficial way does this teaching address our social conduct. I think Jesus was teaching something much more important. Though the New Testament is grounded in the social patterns of first-century Jewish life, the New Testament is about more substantive stuff than saying *please* and *thank you.* I am all for the social amenities; on occasion I have lamented their demise among us. But getting at the sense of the kingdom of God goes far beyond etiquette.

Humility: no Kingdom virtue is more elusive, tricky, slick, now-you-have-it, now-you-don't. So everyone can make the trip, let me take you up the stairs toward the room where humility lives. None of us has gotten all the way into that place. Let's go back to the beginning.

We Begin as Worldlings; We Aggressively Promote Ourselves

Our first nature is take care of ourselves. How can you take care of yourself if you cannot promote yourself? So it seems to me that the businessmen who promote themselves well, do well. Observe the success of some of our car dealers. They go on TV and become gross hucksters. In a kind of bizarre sense they entertain us. They take hucksterism and turn it into a pattern so direct until it becomes funny. But have you noticed one thing about what these people are doing? It works. I do not recall any of those fellows going broke. Since it works, others will surely imitate them.

But let's not knock the car salesmen too much. Watch the way the professional wrestlers taunt and push, call attention to themselves, and boast. Does it work? You know it works. Today we have the Superbowl. The name brands in the game are Theissman and Plunkett, Alzado and Riggins. These people have fit well into the show business atmosphere of professional athletics. Literally, "If you've got it, flaunt it" is the rule of thumb. The result of this boasting and personal salesmanship is athletes who are really big businessmen. They are very wealthy. They have athletic skills, but even more important to their personal fortunes is that they know how to market their athletic skills with a kind of self-promotion.

What the few do before a nation who both envies and admires them, millions more would like to do. The only reason they don't has nothing to do with conscience; they've never had the

opportunity. So little businessmen want to become big businessmen. They are looking for a way to call attention to themselves,
so they can get where they want to go. Little teachers want to
become important teachers. They are looking for a way to move
up. And little preachers are longing, yearning, hungering for a
larger pulpit, a place in the sun. So letters fly, phone calls come,
and convention corridor talk schemes and dreams of ways to
promote and move up.

Built into our nature is the desire to achieve, to win, to do the
best we can. Most people, car salesmen and preachers, businessmen, and government employees want to do this on the basis of
some skill or some ability. Most of us really do argue and
agonize over how we ought to push ourselves. But one way or
another, all of us rationalize until we find a way to promote
ourselves. We have to if we are to live in the world. The best of
us don't like what we have to do. The worst of us never give it
a thought. But the price of getting ahead is "tooting your own
horn." Most of us have reached a sort of accommodation. We
say with a wry grin:

> Verily, verily . . .
> He that tooteth not his own horn,
> That horn shall not be tooted.

If it is a case of toot your own horn or nothing, most of us will
go ahead and toot. Somebody has to sit at the head of the table.
So we reach for the first place. This is our first nature.

We Discover Humility; the Kingdom of God Expects It

Another reality is the world of "me first." At church, from
reading the New Testament, from a book, from watching the
pattern of a friend—somewhere we get the idea of humility. It
is foreign to us, but we recognize something new. Here is a new
way. The idea sticks in the mind. It is tantalizing, attractive. It's
a quality we find at the the heart of the New Testament.

The Sermon on the Mount has three illustrations grouped
tightly. Jesus spoke of *charity*. He said we were to be generous

to both church and the poor. But we are to do that giving in a certain kind of way. "So when you give something to a needy person, do not make a big show of it" (Matt. 6:2). Give, but do not call attention to yourself.

Jesus spoke of *public prayer.* Some of the religious people were making a public spectacle of themselves in their prayers. Jesus said, "When you pray, go to your room, close the door, and pray to your Father, who is unseen. And your Father, who sees what you do in private, will reward you" (Matt. 6:6). Now you see why public prayers in our worship service are so treacherous.

Finally, Jesus spoke of *fasting.* Few of us are into fasting; that is obvious. But the idea is still around the edges of the religious community. It is good if we do not make a show of it. A religious exercise is not a place to call attention to ourselves. That is the sense of the teaching.

Late in the ministry of Jesus his disciples got into an argument among themselves. They were quarreling about who was the greatest. Jesus found out about their argument and made this comment on it: "Whoever wants to be first must place himself last of all and be the servant of all" (Mark 9:35).

Not long after that quarrel Jesus washed the feet of His disciples. You recall the story. When Jesus prepared to wash Simon Peter's feet, Peter would not let Him. It was out of character for the leader to wash the feet of His disciples. But Jesus insisted. In fact, He said the idea of selfless service was to be the ideal of the Kingdom. "I, your Lord and Teacher, have just washed your feet. You, then, should wash one another's feet" (John 13:14).

Paul reflected on the humility of Jesus and said, "Don't do anything from selfish ambition or from a cheap desire to boast, but be humble toward one another, always considering others better than yourselves. . . . The attitude you should have is the one that Christ Jesus had" (Phil. 2:3-5).

That ought to make the point. The Kingdom ideal is that we should put away, graduate out of, grow until we are no longer just self-seeking, self-promoting people of this world. It is not easy. The path is slippery. But the goal is before us. We are to be more and more like Jesus and less and less like horn tooters.

We Fall on Our Faces; False Humility Makes Us Foolish

Now let's imagine we buy into these key New Testament ideas. We know we are supposed to be humble and self-effacing. So we give it a try: *I am no longer going to be a self-promoter; I'm going to be just like Jesus.* We have just set ourselves up. In my personal experience and in some observation of others, it seems to me that most of us who set out to be humble just put on a kind of Halloween mask. Everyone can tell we are wearing a mask. They may not be certain who is behind the mask, but what is advertised is not what they get. It is this very truth that makes the fertile ground for all the humility jokes.

We all know the humility joke that goes like this: a fellow struggled hard with his self-assertion. He tried manfully to be humble. Finally, his peers took note of his struggle and give him a prize for his humility. It was a great button. He had won first prize in the humility contest. But when he put it on, they took it away from him.

The little joke helps to make the point: humility is an elusive quest. Denial of self is a long battle. No quick decision at church, no quiet resolve in privacy puts the matter to rest. And there is a reason for this. At the very center of the Christian faith is the idea of conversion issuing in a new creation. The old person is crucified. Paul put the ideal before us when he said to the Corinthians, "When anyone is joined to Christ, he is a new being; the old is gone, the new has come" (2 Cor. 5:17). I know what I am supposed to be, but I have such a hard time doing it. Is there something wrong with me? Am I not converted? Have I deluded myself when I declared I was a Christian?

As I write this, I'm not speaking of your continuing bouts with a sort of false humility. I am really telling you of my own. Had I not had these struggles, I could not write of them. It helps me to think of the Christian walk as process rather than event. It seems to me some of our religion dangles a sort quick-fix

before us: "Come. Take the step. You will be changed. Now all
your struggles are resolved. You are a new person." Such entice-
ments are well-intentioned, I suppose. But they are not true to
my experience. The Bible tells us of the long journey of the
heroes of faith from self-centeredness to self-giving. It was the
goal, the quest, the stuff of the journey.

If we really set out to deny self, we will encounter some
setbacks. There will be times when we will find ourselves pre-
tending. We may not intend to pretend, but we may do it una-
wares. I suspect we will feel foolish; we betrayed ourselves. But
all this is normal. We are not trying to learn to tie our shoes.
Rather, we have taken on something that is right at the center
of the religious quest. We are wrestling with self. Self does not
die easily.

We Climb Toward the Goal; We Occasionally Forget Ourselves

It seems to me that as long as we are conscious about being
humble, we are not yet humble. True humility cannot happen
until we become self-forgetful. When the great man is unaware
that he is great, then the great man is great indeed. William
Barclay told the story of Thomas Hardy, the English writer-
novelist. Even after Hardy had become very famous, so famous
any paper would compete to run any new thing Hardy might
compose, the great man seemed unaware of his stature. When
he would write a poem he would slip it into a envelope and mail
it to a newspaper. But always in that same envelope Hardy
would put a stamped, self-addressed "envelope for the return of
his manuscript should it be rejected." Just because Hardy had
done well, he wasn't presumptuous. He realized the next pro-
duction might be turned down. Nothing was resting on his
reputation. His work would stand on its own. This is humility.

Losing the self does happen. Charles Wellborn was a soldier
in World War II. He returned to college and seminary about the
same time I was a student. Wellborn told of the soldier-friend
who threw his body upon a grenade that was tossed into their

bunker. The man was blown to pieces, but all of his friends were saved. Is not this some kind of humility? He forgot about himself. In a sense he lost his life for others and for his country. All acts of heroism are really stories about forgetting. The hero forgets about himself. Had he not been able to forget about himself, he could not have done the deed that made him a hero. For heroism is really tipping over the normal standards of life. Instead of taking care of old number one, being a hero is sacrificing self in the interest of a higher cause.

Heroism is usually an act. Self-forgetting for a moment is amazing and commendable. Sometimes I suspect it is a reflex, an unthought act. What makes some do acts of heroism and others cower is hard to unravel. The humility of the New Testament is a by-product of obedience to God. Jesus did not lurch into the cross. It was not a knee-jerk act of self-giving. The thing that has fascinated and drawn us through the centuries toward Christ is the self-giving, the humility, the degradation that was consciously and willingly chosen. He had privileges He did not claim. He had a place, an exalted place, but He did not take it. His humanity and divinity waged war. That is what the garden of Gethsemane prayer is all about. But the self-giving side prevailed. He let himself go. Paul said He gave Himself for us.

The act on the cross was self-sacrifice. But viewed from a larger sense, was it not also a kind of ultimate humility? What He did is what He wants from us. "Whoever loves his own life with lose it; whoever hates his own life in this world will keep it for life eternal" (John 12:25). Let's think about this the next time we reach for the best seats. Come to think of it, if we have to think about it, we aren't there yet.

7
The Great Feast

Luke 14:15-24

A derelict comes into the church office. He is down and out. Life has put him down. He cannot support himself. He has put himself in the position of a beggar. How did he get this way? What went wrong? Most of these people have some ability. Could they be other than they are? If so, how?

The boy has dropped out of college. He has no purpose. His parents are down on him. There is no part of his schooling or work that he can look back upon with pride. The young man is beginning to doubt himself. What he does now is crucial. How can the boy make the right choice? Is there a Bible word to guide him on the way?

A mature woman drops by to talk about marriage. She has not been married before, but now she is considering it. The man she has in mind is not exactly what she had planned for or dreamed of. But he has many attractive qualities. Should she put aside her dreams and some of her treasured values to marry this man? She cares for him. Is there a word from God? What is right?

He is in his mid-thirties. Twice he has turned away from the promotion that would move him up the corporate ladder. But his family is happy here. He loves his friends. He cares about his church. There is a sense of usefulness and service in what he is doing. Should he move on and move up? Should he plant his life here and settle for less in the market and more in family and church? Which way to go?

Neither you nor I can say for sure what these people should

do. In each case there are many considerations to take into account. But in the stories of Jesus there are clues to right conduct and right choices that are timeless. Turning to the Bible will open the wisdom of the ages. Really hearing the stories of Jesus will expose God's intention.

One of Jesus' stories was about a great feast. In Jewish expectation, there was the mental picture of the last day. Heaven had come. God was on His throne. All of His children were gathered around. And the Heavenly Father spread a great feast for all of His children. In the popular expectation of the Jews they would be present, and, probably, they did not expect anyone else to be there. There was a great deal of exclusiveness in the people who gave Jesus trouble. This is the background to the story. And out of the crowd came the statement: "How happy are those who will sit at the feast in the Kingdom of God!" (Luke 14:15). What this man said and what he expected were not exactly what Jesus wanted people to think; so Jesus told a story. The story was designed to correct the popular notion of what God was like and what heaven would be like. But the story is much more.

An Old Agreement

The stories of Jesus make more sense when we understand the ways of the ancient Middle East. Almost lost in this story is this line: "There was once a man who was giving a great feast to which he invited many people. When it was time for the feast, he sent his servant to tell his guests, 'Come, everything is ready!' " (Luke 14:16-17). This part of the story seems a simple introduction to us. But the people who first heard this story heard much more than do we.

Here is what actually happened. The man sent out his servant to invite some special friends to a banquet. The date of the banquet would be set, let's say, for Labor Day. Each person made their choice. They would go, or they would not go. But these people had given their word. They had made an agreement. Now on the basis of these agreements the host proceeds to work toward the day of the party. He buys his food. He makes all of the arrangements for a great feast. He knows who is coming. They have agreed. On the day of the feast when the house and the food are ready, he then sends out his servant with the word: Come now. All is ready for you. On the basis of an agreement the second invitation was extended. To accept the first invitation, then back out on the day of the banquet was an insult. It just was not done. The guest had made an agreement; he was expected to perform on the basis of it. He expected to honor the agreement since the host had gone to such expense and such detail for him.

There is little doubt about what Jesus was saying to the people who heard Him. He was telling them that the Jewish people had entered into a special agreement with God. They were his "chosen people." But when the time came for the Jews to perform for God, they were occupied with other pursuits. Remember the moving passages in Genesis 12 and Exodus 19? In the one, Abraham received the promise of God. In the other, the people entered into covenant with God. This story is set against the background of an old agreement. In fact, all of the Old Testament is set against an old agreement. It is the presupposition that makes sense of all the rest.

To this point all is history. This is a kind of Bible background that is filler: interesting but not earthshaking. However, the Bible will not stay in the past. The words of Jesus are so penetrating, so probing, that they begin to stir the hearts of living people. The God-figure in the story is the host. He has reached out for His children. He wants to give something good to them. I am God's child. He has come to me. I have a reservation made at the great feast in heaven. I have promised to attend. It is an agreement. I made a promise.

I remember the first promise I made to God. I was a boy. When I was ten years old, I promised to be His. I asked forgiveness for my sins. I asked direction for my life. I invited Him into my life. I offered Him control over my life. I was just a boy: I had no idea how much was involved in being God's man in a pagan world. But the agreement was made. I cannot deny it. Buried back in my mind is the clear memory of my baptism and the Bible the church gave me. I entered into an agreement.

Sometimes when I listen to people when they tell of their hard times, I hear them bring up echos of an old agreement. Occasionally, they tell me about the times and the places when they made that agreement. At church we call the agreement our conversion or our salvation experience. But whether we call it by one name or the other, you know what I mean. It is the life-reordering promise we made when we were younger. We promised to come when the Lord God called. Sometimes that promise anchors me. Other times it haunts me. And still other times it pulls me forward.

But there is no time when the agreement is not a factor in how I think about myself and how I act toward God. When I have been wayward, my agreement makes me feel guilty. I hurt. I am ashamed. When I am at a point of decision, I reach back to find direction and balance from my agreement. When I think of the future I am pulled by the invitation that was first a part of the agreement. I am going to a great feast. There's a great day coming. I am invited. I cannot dismiss that old agreement. It is a part of me. Even if you and I have tried to deny our agreement by life or by word, that old promise still exerts a powerful pull on who we are and what we are becoming.

The Pressing Obligations

Right at this point the story turns a corner. Though all the people had agreed to come to the great feast, all of them began to beg off. The first said, "I have bought a field and must go and look at it." The second said, "I have bought five pairs of oxen and am on my way to try them out." And the third, "I have just gotten married, and for that reason I cannot come" (Luke 14:-18-20). So, the three hindrances to honoring their agreement are: possessions, wealth, and pleasures.[1] The old agreement was set aside for the immediate, pressing need of the present.

Time has a way of bending honor. I am promised to God. I

was not coerced into that promise. I made it of my own free will. But the passage of time has dulled the immediacy of my promise. Like the Jews of old, my fields, my oxen, and my family seem much more important to me than an old promise.

Strange. Nothing has changed. The story is just as apropos to us as it was to them. Here we are. We are the promised ones just as the Jews were in the time of Jesus. We still have some sense of the commitment we made. But the agreement is not ordering our lives. We whom God calls do not come. When God gives a chance for service, we are unable to put down the cares of this world for the work of God's kingdom.

And what about you? Will you lay aside some of your work in this world and invest in God's little children? Will you invest in the poor? Will you give yourself to the study and teaching of the Bible? Or do we sing the old song: "I am too tired. I have more than I can say grace over. You just don't know how much I have piled on me now. Come back next year."

And with "one accord, they began to make excuses."

If we order our lives by the pressing, immediate obligations that crowd in on us, we will never have time for God or God's service. This world is an aggressive presence. It crowds us. It lays demands upon us. It puts time binds around us. I have been amused at the way gardening can enslave us. In the spring of the year it seems a garden makes so much sense. We plant expansively. But then July and August come. The garden really does bear generously. Then, what the garden will do to us! We have to put up the peas; they will go to the bad if we do not preserve them. We have to string and freeze the beans. We have to gather, clean, and put up the corn. We have to do it now! If we do not do it now, we will lose it.

Lift this little story out of the immediate. Our lives are so entangled in this life, this world, this work until we must deal with the pressing obligations. They just won't wait. And at the most inopportune time, God comes calling: "Remember that old promise. Now is the day. I need you. Lay down what you are doing and come and invest in Me." The church is but a small shadow of the summons of God. But a shadow of that summons it surely is. If we cannot honor our old agreement in the fellowship of church, what makes us think we will be able to loose ourselves from the concerns of this world by an invitation from an angel?

A Future Relationship

Let's follow the story to the end. The God-figure invites everyone to His feast. And the inclusiveness of the story is a major part of its application. God included the Samaritans and the Galileans and finally even the Gentiles in His feast. That is the way we were invited.

But at the very end of the story there is this threatening line: "None of those men who were invited will taste my dinner!" (Luke 14:24). All of us have trouble with the wrath of God. I know I do. It seems the character of God should always be described as love, patience, and forgiveness. And ample Bible material supports this idea. But Jesus is unpredictable. Some of the most mind-rearranging, troublesome ideas in the Bible come from the lips of Jesus.

If I understand this story, here is what it means: the Jews made a promise to be God's people and do God's work in the world. They became preoccupied with the cares of this world, and when God called them for service and honor they were unable to put down the entanglements of this life. They turned away with lame excuses. God then turned to the unwashed like "the poor, the crippled, the blind, and the lame" (14:21). Finally, His servants were sent out into country roads to "make people come in." Anyone was invited. But what of the people who had first accepted the invitation? "None of those men who were invited will taste my dinner!" (14:24). The lame excuses changed a relationship. God would not have them.

There is some risk is building too much theology on individual stories of Jesus, but surely these stories tell us what God wants us to know of Himself. If I have made an agreement with God at the beginning of life, then I let the cares of this world trap me from the work and will of God, I am jeopardizing my future with God.

We have little to say about heaven. This is not to our credit. But there is going to be a great feast. It is coming. At His own time God is going to send out His messengers into this world to gather His own. But some of us are going to be so busy, so caught up in our property, our ambitions, our money management until we cannot let go and keep our promise to attend the feast. For this we do risk our relationship with God. For when this world becomes too important, this world becomes an idol, a god.

The rich young ruler could not let go his things; he preferred his riches to a future with Jesus (Mark 10:17-22). All of us are like the rich young ruler; we cannot go into His service because we are wed to our things. Let it go. Let it go. Anything we gain in the present is more than lost in the future. For if there is one clear message that leaps from the Bible it is this: keep the promise. It is not just our old promises to God that counts; it is also our future with God that counts. And the tests will always come in the present.

Some of us need to practice the way we are going to respond to God when He calls. In little ways, ways that seem reduced and shrunken, God comes calling. He is asking us to care for the little ones. He may send your minister of education as His angels. He wants us to give up some of ourselves; so He sends a member of the nominating committee. He wants us to test ourselves; so He speaks through the preacher. But in each there runs a common theme: we are denying a part of yourselves to do the work of God. This is preparing us for the greater test that is surely coming. But if we cannot pass the little tests, how can we hope to extricate ourselves from now and things and pleasures. We can't. The church is but a dim shadow of God's call to service, but the church is the clearest shadow of that coming

Kingdom we know. When the church calls, can we answer? How we handle these little tests is preview of the way we will handle the great summons. Think about it. Give a care. A future relationship is on the line.

8
The Lost Sheep

Let me tell you an American story. The clean-cut, all-American boy finishes college. He seeks and finds just the job he wanted. Along the way he met, courted, and won the love of a wonderful girl. Now that he is out of college and has that good job, they can be married.

But the world of work is harder than he thought it would be. He has to put more and more of himself into his job; that means he is putting less and less of himself into wife and children. For a time, only for a time, he reasons, *I have to put my marriage on the back burner of my life. But when I make it up the corporate ladder a few rungs, then I will return to a more reasonable division of my life. I will give more of myself to family.*

So he stays late at the office. The trips out of town come often and last longer. He feels guilty about what he is doing and wishes he were with the children more during these tender years. He promises himself he will not make his wife bear all the responsibility for the family. *Just a little longer and I will be where I want to be in my career,* he reasons.

One day he comes back from an extended business trip. Something is wrong. The pent-up anger his wife has been pushing down has surfaced. She has seen a lawyer and wants a divorce. She is gone and the children with her. He is lost without her.

What happened? He never intended things to come to this. All he wanted to do was get ahead. One of the reasons he wanted to get ahead was for the wife and children. He wanted to provide for them some of the nice things. And now it has all gone wrong.

I have just told you the American version of the story of the lost sheep. Before I go on, here's some background.

Often, Jesus was accused of association with people no devout person should touch. These people were called publicans and sinners. Actually the publicans and sinners were the majority of the population. Only a few folk were Pharisees. The Pharisees were the hard-line, religious people. They took the rules of Moses, fleshed them out to cover a large number of specific situations, then tried to press them down on all people. When most people resisted, the Pharisees declared the people who would not make religion a list of rules were not religious at all. Now we have the background for the opening line of the parable: "One day when many tax collectors and other outcasts came to listen to Jesus, the Pharisees and the teachers of the Law started grumbling, 'This man welcomes outcasts and even eats with them!' So Jesus told them this parable" (Luke 15:1-3).

None of us has the faintest notion of just how strongly the Pharisees felt about separating themselves from sinners. Some of us are straitlaced. Some of us have a little of the puritan in us. We make fun of ourselves with doggerel:

> Rootie titoot, titoot, titoot,
>   We're the boys from the institute;
> We don't smoke, and we don't chew,
>   And we don't go with girls who do.

That we can say such doggerel aloud lets you know we have already escaped the worst of the Pharisee spirit.

Jesus redefined religion. He did not have an easy time doing it. His work is not yet finished in me, for lapsing back into Pharisaism is always a temptation. If I can be good by redefining the rules, I have found a cheap way to do my religion. So I just declare that if my rules are not honored, good religion is not practiced. This makes me good by definition and those who disagree not good. This Pharisaic spirit lurks inside the heart of many devout souls.

Rather than jump upon the highest pedestal and shout,

"You're wrong! You're wrong!" Jesus took another approach. He told a story. The story puts the sinner in a different light. Even more important, the God-figure is made more gentle and loving. Let's look at the lost sheep and the good shepherd.

The Lost Sheep

As a young man I was inclined to believe that all lost sheep willed to be lost. Now that I am a little older and have watched people for a longer period of time, it seems to me George Buttrick is close to the truth in the story he told about an exchange between a farmer and a city man:

> The farmer came down the lane. "Got a stray," he said. How do they get lost?" asked the city man. "They just nibble themselves lost," said the farmer; "they keep their heads down, wander from one green tuft to another, come to a hole in the fence—and never can find a hole by which to get back again." The city man answered, "Like people, like every generation of foolish men."[1]

Most folks don't intend to get lost. They get lost before they know it. They get lost and don't know how they got that way. They are like sheep.

So the girl leaves home, goes to college, dreams dreams. She finishes school and gets a good job. When she was a child she made promises to God. She would be His, would live for Him, do His will and work. But it is a new day for women. Doors are open wide for the alert, hardworking woman. She springs through those doors, moves into a professional role, makes some money, finds friends different from the people she knew when she was at home. One day she casually tunes in a church service on television. The hymns are the same. The Bible readings recall old days and old promises. She thinks about it. Getting where she wanted to go has changed her life. She thought she was on course. In fact, now that she is well-to-do and established, she finds herself lost. She made her fortune and lost her soul. It is an old story. There was no evil plot in the story. It was simply a case of putting our heads down, moving from green tuft to green tuft. And before we knew it, *Where am I? What has happened? I'm lost!*

What's the worth of a lost sheep? In the parable Jesus told of a shepherd who had a flock of one hundred. Ninety-nine were in place; one was lost. This would have been a large flock. Most shepherds did not have so many. In John 10, Jesus described Himself as "the good shepherd" (John 10:11). He says He calls His sheep by name, and the sheep know Him (John 10:3). Throughout John 10, there is a personal relationship between the shepherd and the sheep.

Personal relationships have a way of changing the worth of sheep. This is true until this day. Go to the ranch lands of the West. The cattleman has many cattle. Cattle are a living to him. He buys and sells them. He fattens them and sends them to market for slaughter. Personal relationships count for little with the cattleman. But let's change the story. Let's let the cattleman's daughter find a lame calf, take that calf and nurse it to health, then see how quickly the cattleman can sell that calf. For the daughter's love of the calf, the cattleman will put aside his sale. The calf means something to the daughter. For the daughter he will forget his profit and loss. The calf is known by the cattleman's daughter, and that changes the calf's destiny.

What are we to do with this world's lost sheep? We are not agreed upon an answer to that question. We are arguing.

One group says: *forget the lost sheep* and go home. It is late. There are other things to do. Forget the sheep. Maybe he will wander home just as he wandered away.

A group of Americans says: *replace the lost sheep.* People are treated like spare parts. Parts wear out; people wear out. When they wear out, simply replace them and go on.

From one corner comes the word of some humanitarians: *hide the lost sheep.* They cannot be turned loose in the community. But let's do them no harm. Let's just put them away so they can be safe and out of sight.

Sometimes I think I hear another set of people saying: *do*

away with lost sheep. They have had their chance. They blew it. They made a choice; they endanger society. Let's destroy lost sheep.

From a corner of the company comes a shepherd, the Good Shepherd. Quietly, He sets out to *find the lost sheep.*

All the voices clash. We catch just a word here and there. But the colliding ideas are pulling, lobbying, scheming to win. It is all over lost sheep. Forget them. Replace them. Hide them. Destroy them. Find them. Still the debate goes on. Seems I hear that same debate in the halls of churches. What shall we do with lost sheep? What shall we do with lost sheep? And from inside our own company come the voices: forget them. Replace them. Hide them. Destroy them. Find them. "He leaves the other nine-nine sheep in the pasture and goes looking for the one" (Luke 15:4).

The Good Shepherd

In the summer of 1947, just discharged from the army, I came to Ridgecrest to work on the staff. It was my introduction to the mountains where I've served over twenty years. During that summer one part of the work of the staff was to serve as leader of the hikes some of the guests enjoyed in the afternoon. We would walk all over the mountains.

Not everyone obediently fell into line behind a staffer and took a hike. Occasionally, some would strike out on their own. Two girls had this independent notion one summer afternoon. They went their own way, and soon they were lost. When the evening meal was served, they were not present. Their counselors waited a reasonable time, then they reported the incident to the management. Soon a sizable party was put together to search the mountains to find the lost girls. After midnight, after more than a hundred people had searched for them for more than four hours, two frightened, cold girls were found and brought in. This same story is reenacted each summer in camps and retreat centers all over the the country. Someone is lost; we must go find them.

Why do we look for lost people? It is not our fault they became lost. Let them wait until morning and find their own way back. No. We stop what we are doing, interrupt schedules made months before, and we look until we find them. Why? Some would say it is just human decency. Maybe. But perhaps this is a residue of our former nature. In the beginning we were like the Good Shepherd. An event in Eden damaged us; one can hardly tell we once had a likeness to that of the Son of God. But buried inside us, almost crushed by the weight of the fall, there is still alive another nature. We act like the Good Shepherd. So a city stops while an ambulance hurries to the hospital. The government lets a military plane fly badly wounded a woman cross-country, and no one complains of the cost. Why? It is the Godlike thing to do. We are acting like God acts.

Jesus called himself the Good Shepherd (John 10:11). Let me describe Him as the parable does:

The Good Shepherd risked Himself. Going after one lost sheep sounds simple enough. Why make it out to be something risky? Because it was. Pastureland in Palestine was scarce. The land is uneven. Mountains rise sharply from the sea, linger on a plateau for only a few miles, and then plunge steeply to the crevice that is the valley of the Jordan River. King David was first a shepherd and then king of Israel. Remember his story? He killed a lion and a bear in the course of his shepherd duty (1 Sam. 17:37). So to go for a lost sheep could be treacherous indeed.

But isn't this the whole story of the Bible? The baby in the manger is Jesus coming to find the lost sheep. The wandering preacher is the Shepherd seeking the lost sheep. When He sent out disciples, this was an extension of the Shepherd reaching for his lost sheep. The dying Jesus who hung between heaven and earth is the most graphic of all the pictures of the Shepherd risking Himself for His sheep.

The Good Shepherd persisted until He found His sheep. It is a part of the language of our time to speak of man's search for God. There is a germ of truth in this. All of us have a hunger for God; we quest after Him, though usually we don't know how to put a name on the One we seek. The greater truth of the matter is the other way around. God seeks us. He seeks us through the Good Shepherd. Sheeplike, we are dumb to our need. Something is wrong. We cannot figure it out. We hunger and are not filled, but we have no idea what to do or which way to turn. We are lost.

Is it the story of the human family that we kept after our lostness until we found our way? Not really. Again it is the other way around. The Good Shepherd persisted. Life is like the parable tells it. "He leaves the other ninety-nine . . . and goes looking for the one that got lost until he finds it" (Luke 15:4).

No single parable tells all truth. All parables tell some of the truth. In the story of the lost son, a story we have named the prodigal son, the God-figure waits for the lost son to return. He waits and waits. Finally, the boy comes to himself and returns to his father. In the story of the lost sheep, it is the Good Shepherd who takes the initiative, goes out, and finds the sheep.

The grace of God is more persistent than we realize. All of the Bible story is about a wayward people and a persistent God. So Israel wandered, was rebellious and difficult, but the grace of God stayed after them. In the history of the church, the record of the saints is uneven, but the Good Shepherd has kept on seeking out, saving His own, staying after the last lost sheep.

The Good Shepherd rejoiced in finding His sheep. When Jesus wanted to tie the story of the lost sheep together, He went back to the language and the familiar sayings of His people. The Pharisees were convinced that God wanted to be rid of sinners. So they had a saying, "There is joy in heaven over one sinner who is obliterated before God."[2] Jesus took the very words out of their mouths, changed them ever so slightly, and they came out this way: "I tell you, there will be more joy in heaven over one sinner who repents than over ninety-nine respectable people who do not need to repent" (Luke 15:7).

Sometimes I am not sure church people have the real picture of what Jesus was saying. We are so impressed with bigness and show. But here was a shepherd carrying one little, lost lamb back into to town. And this caused rejoicing in heaven? Why? Heaven has different ideas about worth than we do. If there had been a thousand lambs that might have been cause for rejoicing, but this was only one. Maybe the church needs to change its focus. Instead of bigness and show, might we not come nearer the Bible if we risked, persisted, and rejoiced over the one?

When all is said and done, the Lord rejoices over the reclaiming of His lost children—one at a time. As each lamb has value, so each fallen child of God has value. Heaven is watching. Each time the Good Shepherd finds one of us, heaven rejoices. It's nice to know heaven cares when one of us comes home.

9
The Lost Son

Luke 15:11 24

The story of the prodigal son has been the subject for so many sermons until it would appear that all has been said that can be said about it. In fact, this story is one of the best known short stories in literature. In the popular mind "the prodigal" has come to mean a debauched, dissolute fellow. The skid row bum, the convicted criminal, the irresponsible tramp: these are prodigal types. There is a sense in which this is true, but there is a larger sense in which this popular definition of the prodigal has stolen from the story its usefulness.

Most of us can easily factor ourselves out of the first part of the story. We do not see ourselves as prodigal. We hope this book will find its way to other readers—as far as this chapter is concerned. We hope some prodigals somewhere read and heed it. But we are excepted and excused. The reason is simple: we are not prodigals.

A lot that has been said and written about prodigal living has been off target. To dwell upon the ugliness of the prodigal's sins is to shift the thrust of the story. Most of us have not lived out all our ugly fantasies. So we dismiss the story as having application to us.

But what if the story were put to us differently. Suppose the tendencies in the prodigal that made him to do what he did were brought to light. What if we look beyond the prodigal's deeds to his attitudes and motives? You see, I think there are more prodigals than we have been willing to admit. By defining a prodigal as one who is debauched we have gotten ourselves out of this story, for most of us are not debauched. Had we defined the prodigal as one who was willful and wrongheaded in his youth, well that's a different matter. I suspect a number of us could crawl back into the story.

When correctly understood, most all of us have lived out the sequence of moods and experiences, the fantasies, and disillusionments of the prodigal. But there is one notable difference: most of us have not finished the story. Jesus tied His story together. It ends right. All the parts fall into place. The boy comes to himself. The Father waits for the boy. The boy tries to make his speech. The Father will have none of it. There is celebration. The lost son has come home. Sins are forgiven. There is rejoicing in heaven. Identity has been restored.

Let us explore all the parts of the story, find the place where we get off and where we are stuck. But best of all, let's stay together to the end. If we can finish *our* prodigal story, we can know the joy of homecoming, too. And that is what Christian faith is all about: getting back in touch with the loving Father.

Wrongheadedness

Getting from childhood to maturity is a course is filled with obstacles, uncertainties, even dangers. In fact, some never make it though they live to be seventy. Even in childhood there come the stirrings of assertiveness and self-will that are both positive and negative. Taken in the right way, these stirrings of self-will are necessary. The child needs to grow up, leave home, and become an independent, self-supporting human being.

Controlling the adolescent desire for independence is hard. Twist the mind just a little, and what comes out is not a necessary desire for self-expression and independence; rather, what one gets is a self-willed, wrongheaded, inexperienced teenager. Out of the story jumps this character we all know.

A man had two sons. The younger boy was now eighteen. He had worked for his father in the business for several years. He had done the menial chores and the dirty work. As he watched and learned, he began to second-guess his father. He thought he had better ideas. When those ideas were put to his father, the father would not respond. The boy's creativity had been rejected. Besides, he was the second son. By Jewish law the second boy would inherit only half as much as the first son. So there was no future for the younger son. He was condemned by birth to a small inheritance. He had been condemned from birth to a menial place.

There is another suggestion in the story. It is not baldly stated, but around the edges of the text there are some hints. It appears that the Father ran a clean house; some discipline was expected from the people who lived with the father. The first son did not seem to mind this discipline; the second son chafed under it. Discipline had always been a bad word to him. Get the picture: an older brother who is too straight; a father who seems too strict; a future without fun! So the boy said, "Give me mine; I'm leaving" (paraphrase of Luke 15:12-13).

I never said to my father, "Give me mine; I'm leaving." No son in our culture asks for his inheritance when he is eighteen. But another part of the story I know firsthand. The tendency to rebel, the flight from authority, the desire to escape: these are feelings I had. Sometimes my parents told me I was not to do thus and so; to me it made no sense that I should be denied the right to do thus and so. I resented their suppression of my reasonable requests. I was no longer a child. Why should I be treated as one? By the time I left for college I harbored considerable resentment toward my parents. I felt cooped up, unduly restrained by just the normal life style of our home. I saw no chance to change the life-style of our home; I was glad for a decent way to make my exit. I did not just *go* away to college. I *ran* away to college.

We dismiss such attitudes as normal. He is just a "normal youth." She is just a "strong-willed girl." There is some truth in what we say. But that is not the whole of it. There is risk in prodigal wrongheadedness. Risk is not sin. But wrongheadedness will make a youth do wrong things he would not otherwise do. The prodigal spirit has an "I'll show 'em" quality in it. Any

parent who has learned anything while growing up knows that
the wrong company, a few beers, and a reckless driver spells
risk.

In the introduction I said so many of us dismiss ourselves
from the prodigal story. It does not apply to us. We have never
been prodigals. To this point in the story can you identify with
the boy? I can. In fact, in some ways it is my story.

Wastefulness

I wonder how the father came up with a third of his holdings.
I suspect he went to the bank, signed a note on his business, and
took the cash and gave it to his son. Imagine being asked to
come up with one third of your estate on short notice! But the
father did it. All at once two strong currents were running
through the mind of the father: my son is about to do a very
foolish thing; I cannot keep my son from doing what he wills
do. Imagine the pain of the father as he saw his son off.

But off he was. It was away to the "far country" (Luke 15:13,
RSV). Things haven't changed much. Jesus told this story, and
the people who heard it probably imagined a young Galilean
making his way to the big city of Jerusalem or perhaps even
Babylon. In our imagination we can see the boy from a small
town going to a distant big city, or the girl from a nearby city
going to New York or Los Angeles. Our literature has the kid
from Iowa going to New York to try his hand at the big city.
Sometimes these people have gone to make their fortune. Sometimes they have gone as prodigals. They are drawn to the bright
lights, and they are escaping parents they see as repressive.

Happily the Bible story does not dwell upon or give the details
of the squandered money and the loose living (Luke 15:13,
RSV). It must have been a short trip on the fast track. Fair-
weather friends crowded around him to help him spend his
inheritance. Surely the boy was insecure; he picked up too many
big checks. He had to impress his friends that he could pay his
own way; so he paid his own way and theirs. But that kind of
life can spend money fast. Stay in a fine hotel in New York for

a month, eat at the posh restaurants every night, go down to Atlantic City and gamble a little, take in the sporting events, have a week in Rome and a fortnight in England—and to make it all more fun, take along some "friends" as your guests. No amount of money can stand that kind of waste for long. Soon it was gone.

Still the point of the story is not the sinful living; the Bible story dwells upon *the waste of it all.* Literally, to be prodigal means "given to wasteful extravagance; . . . characterized by wasteful expenditure; lavish," (according to *Webster's Collegiate Dictionary*.) Here is where so many of us preachers have missed the mark. To dwell upon the sins of the prodigal as he wasted his substance makes for lurid preaching. To dwell upon the waste of it all is biblical preaching. Through and through, the Bible is opposed to waste. We have seen this in earlier chapters. Jesus could not bear the servant who let his one talent just lie idle in the ground. He condemned such waste and idleness. When the fig tree would not bear, Jesus cursed it (Mark 11:13). It was good for nothing; it cluttered the ground. Our Puritan fathers were near to the point of the Scriptures when they taught that waste was a sin. So the slogan: "Waste not; want not."

Still all of this is almost beside the point. To waste a plant or a dollar is one thing. To waste a life is something else. I recall a wasted time in my life. I had escaped home and parental control. I was at Baylor in fall of 1945. Soon I would be going to the army. I was new at college. What a joy to be on my own! Of course the point of going to college was to go to class. Hopefully, I would learn something. But class was the dullest part of the day. The people, the activities, the going, the doing— these were the real and exciting times. Class was much like life back home. I was supposed to do this, read that, study for a test, and write a paper. It was boring and hard; underlying it all there was the call for discipline. I would have none of it.

I recall with great clarity the day I was in Rena Mars McLean Gymnasium playing basketball. It was 2:30 in the afternoon. My

English class was at 2:40. I knew I had to leave if I were to be on time. I made a calculated decision: I would cut this English class. I was not sick. I had no valid reason. I just did not go. I did not keep the appointment. It was a prodigal time in my life.

The last week in February, 1946, I was taking second-quarter finals. On March 11, I would report to Fort Sam Houston. *What difference does it make whether I study for finals,* I reasoned, *I'm going to the army anyway. By the time I get back who will know what grades I made?* Steve Wheeless, Harold Hall, Bill Simpson, and I played dominoes until 12:30 in the morning. Then we had to go out and get some food before we could study. By the time we got back from the Elite Cafe it was 1:30 in the morning. I put my mind to Dr. Steven's chemistry course. But soon I was very sleepy. You should not be surprised to know that in chemistry I had my only D in college. It was a prodigal time—a time of waste. It was a throwaway part of my life.

Jesus does not bear down on the ways the boy wasted his life. We can waste our lives in ways that will offend no one. We need not drink, gamble, or run around. Waste is its own sin. And to waste time and the good things that could be made of time, this is the waste Jesus condemns. In 1945 a movie came out about alcoholism called *The Lost Weekend.* Some of us have lost months, years. We were not drunk. We were just playing through life. The prodigal ran out of money; happily, he did not run out of time. If we run out of time, all is lost.

It may be that we are in the prodigal time of life. We may be just coasting, going nowhere, drifting. God did not make us and invest in us to see us wasted. If we are Christ's, we are to be about good things. Duty, discipline, dedication—these are the words that made us run away from the father in the first place. Our Heavenly Father gives grace and forgiveness when He lets us come back home. But home will always have duty, discipline, and dedication. A great part of the meaning in life comes from those words.

Loneliness

One part of the prodigal story has been given small place. When the boy had spent all his money and when a famine had come upon the land, he joined himself to "one of the citizens of that country" who gave him the job of feeding the swine (Luke 15:15, RSV). Jews had such low opinion of swine that they would not even call them by name. They simply referred to pigs as "the other thing."[1] We know the boy was about to starve, or he would not have taken the work.

He had spent all his money. His fair-weather friends had deserted him. He was now about to starve. To complicate matters there was a recession and a famine in the land. He was reduced to feeding "the other things." Now he was eating the "pods that the swine ate" (Luke 15:16, RSV). But there is one more line: "And no one gave him anything" (Luke 15:16, RSV). I suspect this was the hardest part of all for the prodigal.

You see, the prodigal had grown up in a different kind of a home; he was his father's son. In his father's house there was compassion for the helpless. Tenderness, love, a sense of obligation for the poor—these were the ways of the house. This was the way his father was. Probably the boy had never really been vulnerable; he had been protected in his father's house. He had been protected by the wealth he had in his rich days. But now he was exposed. Now he was learning about a different kind of people. They take, but they don't give. They stick with one when one is flush; they run out on a friend when one is broke.

Perhaps you grew up in the gentle and loving home of the father. But you have gone away. You did not go away into debauched living. You embraced foreign gods. You are not feeding swine; you are doing the treadmill work. You have a living, but you have no life. In your teen years you learned all the doubts that have discredited your childhood faith. Now you are faithless and prudent. You are clothed in body but naked in soul. It is a poor way to live. You have steak and and all the trimmings for the flesh; you have pods and husks for the spirit.

You have learned the hard way that the essence of life is not in the things you possess. You have them, but they are not what you really want. You want meaning in life! You want purpose in life! You want to be a part of great causes!

It's lonely out there. You delighted in the heady thoughts that stripped from you the faith of your father. It was the spending of the inheritance that was rightfully yours. You squandered it; counted it as of no value. But now that it is gone, what have you? Where are all the clever fellows who debunked the ways of the simple house where you grew up? Have they nothing to give you to live on? Beware those who strip you but give you nothing.

Discovery

Get the picture? The boy was lonely and hungry. He was humiliated by the work he was doing. He sat down and thought about his condition. This may have been the first time the fellow had really taken stock of what had happened to him. He reviewed the conditions of his life. He thought of the condition of the servants in his father's house. Even the servants were treated with courtesy and kindness. But here he was alone and humiliated—just barely able to keep body and soul together. Had his father told him these things before he went from home, he would not have believed him. But now he had learned. There really are people who do not care about you. There really are people who will use you. But there is a different kind, too. There were people like his father. And the boy made a discovery about himself as he sat in the pigpen. *I am like my father; I am not like those people. They are not what I am about. They are not my kind of people. I'm going to get up and go home to my father. I am what he is; he is what I hope to be.*

William Barclay said it well.

Jesus paid sinning mankind the greatest compliment it has ever been paid. "When he came to himself," said Jesus. Jesus believed that so long as a man was away from God and against God he

was not truly himself; he was only truly himself when he was on
the way home.[2]

"He came to himself" is the discovery all of us need to make.
But the strange part of it is that the boy thought he was himself
when he was in the far country. He was the boy who liked the
high life. He may have said, "I'm just doing my thing." Or, "I
gotta be me!" But when it was all said and done, the high life
was not the real life for the prodigal. He was living in illusion
when he was in the far country. He was in reality when he was
at home. This illusion still escapes millions of us. We fancy that
if only we could escape, there we would find living. Escape *is*
illusion. Reality is at home in service, duty, discipline. And what
a way to learn about ourselves. He had to learn it all the hard
way.

Do you know who you are? Some of you have thought you
were meant for the high life and the fast track. You thought you
were meant to run with the beautiful people. But who are you?
Are you one of them or are you your Father's child? Finding
out who you are is one of life's great discoveries. All the while
this troubled, restless boy had been his father's boy. In his
waywardness he had betrayed "his deepest self."[3] You cannot
live at peace when you are not being who you are.

Church is meant to take us to self-discovery. The Father-
figure still waits. The children still play out their prodigal days.
But for some there comes the moment of discovery. We call it
grace. The hidden things about who we are come to the top. We
see ourselves. We are meant for relationships that are lasting.
We are our Father's children. We discover ourselves, and we
begin the journey home.

10
The Elder Brother

Luke 15:25-32,

The previous chapter was about The Lost Son. How good it
would be if the story ended on the high note of the return of the
prodigal. It does not. There follows a second parable: the story
of the elder brother. Some commentators have tried to make us
believe that the additional paragraph about the elder brother
was added later. There is no real evidence to support this. And
further, the story hangs together. The last part, the part about
the elder brother, rings true to life. We have all known "elder
brothers." So let us not put away the powerful teaching of the
elder brother parable. Rather, let us learn from it.

When Jesus spoke the story of the elder brother, He almost
certainly was aiming the truth of the story at the self-righteous
Jews who so harassed His ministry. Not all the Jews were self-
righteous. But the people who gave Jesus the most trouble were
the earnest, long-faced, straight-living, never-forgiving Pharisees. Jesus was a problem for these people. He ate with publicans
and sinners. He attracted the common people (Mark 12:37). His
nearest followers were fishermen who were untrained in the fine
points of the Law. Little rules so important to Pharisees were
put aside by Jesus. He lived a freer, more unrestricted, happy,
open life. These ways of Jesus offended the Pharisees.

But that was not the nut of the matter. When some of the
prodigal types began to repent and follow Jesus, Jesus did not
lay heavy rules upon them and make them grovel to get back
into God's good graces. Rather, He welcomed them home and

rejoiced at their newfound faith. He made a large place for them in His mission.

All of this had a powerful impact upon the Pharisees. They weren't glad about the ministry of Jesus. They disagreed with the gospel of Jesus. And they did not count His converts as "really converted." The Pharisees were the elder brothers. When wayward Jews came back home under the preaching of Jesus, Pharisees did not receive them gladly. They gave them the elder brother treatment. When Gentiles tried to come into the Kingdom, Gentiles were again frozen out or made to worm their way into the company of the holy. So when the parable was first spoken, it had a hard-hitting message for the religious establishment of the Jews. Jesus invited all the prodigals back home. The pharisaical Jews weren't happy with their return.

History is great to know, but history can be an escape. Now that we know about the sins of the Pharisees, is that the sum of the matter? I think not. The truth of the matter is that most church-going people are more likely to sin like the elder brother than like the prodigal.

He Minds the Store

Surely you can identify with the feelings of the elder brother. Get the picture: there is a younger brother who does not like to do his part about the family farm. He loafs, laughs at the necessary chores, and lets everyone know his contempt for his father's estate. Finally, the boy's words are acted out. He really does ask his father for his part of the inheritance, converts it to cash, and goes to the bright lights of the big city. What the prodigal does with his inheritance is left largely to our imagination, but what the elder brother does is spelled out in the parable. "Lo, these many years I have served you, and I never disobeyed your command" (Luke 15:29, RSV).

So back home, month in and month out, spring and summer, fall and winter, the elder brother does the work. If he has cows, he has to milk them. If he plants a crop, there comes a time when he has to harvest. It is not flashy work, but it is the stuff of a stable society. Elder brothers are the solid citizens who carry the town. They pay the taxes, serve on the boards and committees, and run the volunteer agencies. They sell the soda pop at the high school football game, coach the kids in little league, and go door to door for various charities. Elder brothers are not dragged into court for income tax evasion; they pay theirs. Elder brothers keep the church going. They pay the tithes. One can't run a church on the erratic gifts and ways of the prodigal. Elder brothers create estates, run banks, provide a stability, a continuity that is necessary.

It is stylish to mock the elder brother and point up his faults. They are legion, but there is a quality about the elder brother that is not to be mocked. What would the father have done without him?

Yet the virtues of the elder brother were his undoing. The very quality that made him content to stay at home and do the menial work was given just a little twist and came out as a sin. The boy came to think that staying at home was of the essence of goodness. His straight, hardworking pattern of life became the part of his nature he was most proud of. It would appear that the boy reasoned like this: *I am not like my brother. He is away in Los Angeles wasting his inheritance; I am home enlarging mine. What my brother is doing is evil and wrong; what I am doing is good and right.*

Put under an objective light, I hope you can see the subtlety in the boy's reasoning. Is it better to stay at home and work for your father than to go into the far country and waste your inheritance? The answer has to be yes. So is the one son the more responsible, the more to be commended than the other? Again, the answer has to be yes. But somewhere something went wrong. "While the younger son was prodigal in body, at least part of his heart was always at home; but the elder brother was prodigal at heart, and only his body was at home."[1]

Quietly, almost insidiously, the elder brother had come to think that his staying at home was the essence of goodness. He was good because he was not like his brother. He was good because he was obeying his father. He was good because he did not do public, raunchy sins. All of this kind of thinking is the way legalists think. It is into this pit that the Pharisees fell. Paul would battle this frame of mind as he tried to start churches among the Jews and Gentiles of the Mediterranean world.

Avoiding the sin of the elder brother is harder than you think. You were probably in church Sunday. Is that good? I hope so. Is it better than not being in church? True. We are commanded to go to church. But going to church, going to Sunday School, tithing, living out our religion in daily life while a virtue can become the ground of our own undoing. We come to see ourselves as good because we do all of these things. The essence of true religion is found in another place.

The real wealth of the elder brother was in a relationship. He was his father's son. Therein was the real source of his future. When the younger son "came to himself" in the pigpen, he realized his relationship to his father. The elder brother had lost the sense of his security and his wealth. The father reminded him saying, "Son, you are always with me, and all that is mine is yours" (Luke 15:31, RSV). But there is no record that the boy heard his father's words. "Self-righteousness is sin as well as unrighteousness, and may be even a worse sin."

He Forgets His Sin

I have read this text very carefully searching for one hint that the elder brother was aware of any sin in himself. It is not there. "While the younger son confesses with no excuse, the elder son boasts with no confession."[3] The man seems to be unaware of, impervious to, his sin. He can list the sins of his brother. "When this son of yours came, who has devoured your living with harlots" (Luke 15:30, RSV). He can accuse the father saying, "You never gave me a kid, that I might make merry with my friends" (Luke 15:29, RSV). But he has no thought that he might be in need of forgiveness too.

But it is right here that the sins of the elder brother are so elusive, so subtle. There is a kind of self-deception here. Compared to the life-style of the younger brother, how could the older brother keep from thinking he was good and responsible? Yet this is where the Christian religion becomes hard. Just as soon as we escape the sins of the flesh, we are the more likely to be victim to the sins of the spirit. Which is the greater sin: To go into a far country and waste inheritance in riotous living? Or to stay at home feeling smug about the virtue that is yours— not going into the far country and wasting your inheritance? The one is the sin of the prodigal; the other is the sin of the elder brother. Both are sins. Here are some of the sins of the elder brother:

Bitterness and anger. As soon as the elder brother learned his brother had come home, he was angry. "He was angry and refused to go in" [to the feasting and the dancing and music] (Luke 15:28, RSV). It would appear that man was seething, boiling, stewing inside about the unfairness of life. We cannot help but speculate that the elder brother wished he had taken his inheritance and gone into the far country. Was the younger brother only living out the fantasies of the older brother?

Why the celebration? There ought to be punishment. If there were justice, there would be punishment. He deserves it. Or so his attitude seemed to be. He was a man filled with a bitter kind of anger.

Self-pity. In the accusation thrown in the face of the father there is the sure sign of self-pity. "Lo, these many years I have served you, and I never disobeyed your command; yet you never gave me a kid, that I might make merry with my friends" (Luke 15:29, RSV). Here is the poor fellow who had no fun. All he had done was stay home and do the chores. But while he did the chores, his mind was turning: *Why doesn't the old man recognize what I am doing for him? There is no reward for goodness and faithfulness. Why does he not notice and praise me?* And on and on his mind went, feeling sorry for himself. The younger brother had fun. The older brother had no fun.

Self-pity saps any beauty we have in us. A friend made a happy response to my question: "How are you?" He said, "Well,

I'm all right. I could tell you my troubles, but it would do no good, and you don't want to listen to them anyway." Not a bad line. All of us have our aches and pains. All of us have been put upon. All of us have been slighted at one time or the other. The capacity to shuck it off and get on with the business of life is the sign of good mental health and good religion. The good things that have come my way far outweigh the bad. Beware the debilitating sin of self-pity. It will make you a whiner.

Insensitivity. There is no record in the story that the elder brother ever felt the hurt and the pain of the younger brother. He did not bother to find out. When the prodigal hurt in the pigpen, the elder brother did not hurt with him. When the father grieved over the life-style and the departure of the prodigal, there is no record that the elder brother entered into the father's grief. His was a kind of contorted goodness. He was sure that the hurt that had come to his brother was well deserved. He did not hurt with him; he was glad that sin was now being punished.

Yet there is a course that could have been taken by the elder brother that would have changed all of the story. What if the elder brother had gone out into the far country, looked for, found, and persuaded the prodigal to come home before he was so bruised and hurt and wounded by his sin. He had no compassion. He didn't have the grace of sensitivity.

Bitterness, anger, self-pity, and insensitivity: what a list of sins! Yet there was no confession in him. He could list the sins of others. He was unaware he had any of his own. But what had changed?

Are we not the same? We can rattle off the vices and the foibles and the follies of our neighbors, but we cannot see our own. Sin is that way. It blinds us to our own needs while directing us to the faults of others.

He Refuses an Invitation

Almost lost to the story is the act of the father. When the elder brother learned of the celebration for his brother, he was angry. Somehow word came to the father that his firstborn was not present. He went outside to invite him in. The text goes further than my words. The Bible story says, "His father came out and entreated him" (Luke 15:28, RSV). He begged him, implored him, beseeched him. But there is no record that the elder brother ever accepted the father's invitation.

I know the kind of fellow we are talking about. He knows how to be righteous and correct. He does not know how to have a good time. In fact, he is more moral than he is decent. All celebration is suspect. Had there been a session on the ills of the country or the sins of the younger generation, this man would have been an authority. But when the time came for the kind of joy and genuine delight at the return of the wayward one, the elder brother was lost.

Debunking Puritans is not my thing. It seems to me that there was more good in the Puritans than we have ever seen. But one side of the puritanical character was that they did not know how to go to a party. In fact, frivolity was preached against. Partying, so popular and acceptable today, was out in Puritan New England.

If the elder brother had taken the father's invitation and gone inside, he would have been expected to embrace the prodigal and tell him he was glad that he had come home. Such words would have been so outside his spirit that he could not bring himself to go inside and tell a lie. It would almost appear that the elder brother would have preferred that the prodigal not come home.

The man missed a chance for reconciliation, and reconciliation is what the Bible is all about. Let's keep the big story in view. In the Garden of Eden we are told that the human family disobeyed God, was cursed, and then put out of the garden. In Christ at Calvary, God made a way for reconciliation. What had been estranged can now come home. What had been out of joint now fits. What had been separated is now together again. With Paul we can all say, "All this is from God, who through Christ reconciled us to himself and gave us the ministry of reconciliation; that is, in Christ God was reconciling the world to himself,

. . . and entrusting to us the message of reconciliation" (2 Cor.
5:18-19, RSV). Reconciliation is what the Christian religion is
all about. Here was a man who did not glory in reconciliation.
Here was a man who would rather perpetuate his disdain and
contempt for his brother than to put them away and come be
reconciled. This is the opposite of God's way.

Whether we can accept the invitation of the Father and go
inside and welcome the prodigal—this is a test. The prodigal's
test came in the pigpen. The good news is that he "came to
himself." But still unresolved by the story is the fate of all the
elder brothers. The prodigal was home. The party was in
progress. But the elder brother was outside. Strange as it seems,
it was not the prodigal who missed life; he had seen more of life
than he planned to see. It was the elder brother who missed the
party. God is having a party. There is rejoicing in heaven over
the ones who have come home (see Luke 15:7). Everybody is at
the party. Everyone except the elder brother. All the elder
brothers not only miss the sin and the pain, elder brothers miss
God's great homecoming party. It seems to me, missing God's
homecoming party is too high a price to pay for a little self-
righteousness. Why not do away with the charade of self-righteousness. Come on in. Welcome the prodigal home. Forgive
and forget. God is having a party, and you are invited.

11
The Loving Father

Luke 15.11-32

It is hard for us to know what God is like. This is not because God is strange so much as it is because God is other than we are. Inscrutable, mysterious, incomprehensible—these are some of the words used to tell about God.

In my ministry, I am confronted with this truth week after week. Some time ago I called a woman whose husband had just died of a heart attack at age fifty-four. She was heartbroken. In the course of our brief conversation, as I tried to tell her of our pain and our share in hers, she said, "I just can't understand it; we had so many plans and dreams not yet lived. I don't know God's plan; I just don't understand."

Allow me to offer another illustration. It is not offered as sacrilege; in fact, it is offered with holy purpose. Have you ever tried to figure out what an animal might be thinking? We have a cat. Sometimes when I am doing yard work, I sit down to rest. There is Elsa, our cat. Elsa has lived at our house for nearly seventeen years. I know when Elsa is hungry. Dot can tell when Elsa is sick. But to carry this a step further, does Elsa think? If Elsa thinks—and it seems to me that she does—what does she think? All sorts of experiments have been undertaken to determine the intelligence of animals. Some of these have given us a measure of insight into the way animals think. But no one knows for sure. No one has ever voluntarily abandoned humanity and entered into catness, taken on the form and the limitations of a cat. Such a transformation would be miraculous. To do it would defy all the rules of the physical world. That anyone should want to do it would make that one suspect. What risks! Every dog would be out to chase you. Your life span would be something like ten to twenty years if you could dodge the cars for that long, stay near a friendly vet, and find someone who would feed you. But not until then would you know what it is like to be a cat.

Now let's carry this little story one step further. Suppose while I am sitting there thinking about what Elsa is thinking, Elsa is sitting there thinking about what I am thinking. Elsa has to live with human beings. They are the ordering force in her life. She has to come to terms with us. We are bigger. We bring in the cans of cat food. We decide whether she stays in the house or stays out in the rain or cold. Though she does not understand why we do what we do, she has to adapt, fit into, and come to terms with us. We are in charge. But though we are in charge, that does not make it easy for Elsa to understand. We are always a mystery to Elsa.

Now let's go back and pick up an earlier thought: It would be amazing should anyone want to take on catness, enter into the life and the body of a cat, accepting the limitations and the risks of a cat. If someone was able to be transformed into a cat, then where would be the best place for Elsa to get inside information about what humans were like? If only Elsa could find that cat, the one that really had the mind and the spirit and thought processes of a human being, then Elsa would have her best chance to know what people are thinking. She would be learning about being human from a cat who had been human.

There is more difference between God and people than there is between me and my cat. No one knows God. To speak of knowing God is to speak of glimpses, fleeting snatches of insight into the ways of the Almighty. Barry White speaks of the God who is so beyond us this way: "All of our words about God are but fences around a mystery."

But do not jump to the wrong conclusion. If God is so hard to know, why bother? Let Him be. Forget it. Go on about your business and quit trying to figure out that which cannot be

known. That is not really an option. It would be like Elsa saying
she was going to give up on Dot and me. That is one of her
options, but it is such a devastating one. She could run away,
try it on her own, wander up and down the alleys looking for
waste food. She could hunt the birds and the squirrels. But have
you ever seen one of those cats? They are lean, starved, and wild.
They are out of sorts with the rulers of their world. You can take
that approach, but it is a hard way to go. So Elsa needs to try
to learn to understand us. And we need to try to understand
God.

Are there any clues? Is there any way we can reach across and
know what God is like? In the New Testament there is a story
that is altogether amazing. It tells of a God who loved people
so much and worried about the wasting and wild ways of people
so much that He voluntarily sent a part of Himself and let that
part of Himself enter into humanity. Now I do not understand
this. If I were to make such a move, all of me would be involved
in the transfer. That is, if I were to take on catness, no part of
me would be held back from the commitment to catness. But
for our understanding, the New Testament tells us that God's
Son came in the form of a man. "The Word became flesh and
dwelt among us, full of grace and truth; we have beheld his
glory, glory as of the only Son from the Father" (John 1:14,
RSV).

If you want to get the best of all insights into the mind of God,
a mind we can but partially understand at best, where should
we look? Ought we not look to the One who has been God, who
understands God, is in true nature Godlike? This same question
was put to Jesus by one of His disciples. Philip said, " 'Lord,
show us the Father, and we will be satisfied.' Jesus said to him,
'Have I been with you so long, and yet you do not know me,
Philip? He who has seen me has seen the Father' " (John 14:8-9,
RSV).

Here is the great message of the church: if we want the best
insight into the mind of God, a mind we can but partially
understand at best, we look to Jesus. He is our only hope for

knowing the unknowable. It is Jesus who has come from that other realm, that other dimension of life. Jesus has entered into humanity, "taking the form of a servant, being born in the likeness of men" (Phil. 2:7, RSV). It is He who brings us our most authoritative word from the God who is other. Now do you see why we sing about Jesus? It is He who gives us a crack in the door, a narrow shaft of light into the unknowable.

Jesus spoke to us in stories and deeds. Both in what He said and what He did we learn what God is like. The best of these stories is the story about the loving father. No story can make simple that which is not simple. No story can tell all. No story has all theology wrapped in it. But in the story of the loving father we get the kinds of clues we have to have to make it. It is unfair to expect to know all about God. But it is so necessary to know something about God, for we live in a God-ordered world. If we would live and do well, we must come to peace with our Father. Just as if Elsa would live and do well, Elsa must come to terms with me and my wife.

What does the story of the loving Father tell us about the nature of God? Can we understand it? Does it help? You decide.

The Loving Father Has Two Needy Sons

As I have studied this story, one truth that had previously escaped me has come home with great force: the loving father has two needy sons. Read the story with care, and you will see that just about as much time is spent in helping and healing the faults of one as the other.

I think Jesus is telling us something we have not yet heard. Prodigal and elder brother want to fight among themselves. Both want to compare themselves to each other. The one says, "I am not a Victorian prig and a straight arrow like my brother." While the other says, "I am not a prodigal and a drifter like my brother." And each criticism is beside the point. Both brothers are in trouble. Both have missed the mark. Both are in sin. And both are in need of the healing care of their Father.

Consider this: both are sons; both are brothers; both are

needy; both are stewards. For all of us have to come to terms
with God. Whether we spend our days prowling the far country
or spend our days at home minding the store, we still have to
settle up with the Father. The Father owns the farm we live on.

The Loving Father Forces Nothing

There is a kind of restraint practiced by the loving father that
is both fearful and wonderful to behold. This restraint is both
one of the wonders and one of the mysteries of the story. With
the younger son the father had to practice his restraint in two
ways.

He did not want the boy to go from home. The father knew
the far country was filled with charlatans and crooks and fair-
weather friends who would fleece his boy. He also knew that not
everyone who went into the far country lived to return. The far
country does not place a high value on the life of a country boy
with a little money. The boy left home against the father's
wishes, but the father let him go. He would not keep the boy if
the boy did not want to stay.

And again, while the boy was gone from home—and it must
have seemed an eternity to the Loving Father—the father did
not organize a posse to go out and find the boy and bring him
to his senses. Rather, the Father just waited. He waited until the
boy "came to himself" (Luke 15:17). What restraint. What
self-control. Have you ever waited for your child to come home
from a date on a dark, cold night? I have. Now it is one o'clock.
Now half-past one. Where could she be? Should I do something?
If I can think thoughts like this, how much more can the Author
of all life be restless at our wayward ways. For remember, He
is not the dispassionate father. He is the Loving Father.

But the older boy called forth restraint from the father, too.
Remember when the father went outside to beg his older boy to
come in and be reconciled with his brother? The father stood
there and explained, said his great appreciation for the elder
brother, and begged him to come in and be reconciled and
celebrate. But the older brother would not come in. He chose

a stubborn self-righteousness to a happy reconciliation. And the father's real wishes were frustrated.

At no point in the story did the father force the boys. He had wishes. His love and affection were plain to see. But he did not force his boys. If this story is a real insight into the character of God, what does this story tell us about God? How does it help us to understand our world?

A lot of things happen in our world that displease our Heavenly Father. To blame or saddle God with an accounting for all the sadness and suffering that takes place in our world is misguided. How much of our suffering has been caused by prodigal living? God only knows, but a large part of our pain is self-inflicted. Sometimes shortness of life or shortness of breath come from choices we have made. It is not the will of God; it flies in the face of God's will.

Now here's the other side of the coin: How much pain is there in our world as a result of elder brothers? These are the people who insist that wrong be punished, prodigals stay prodigals, and justice be done.

The notion that full justice can only be meted out by God is a humbling thought. But elder brothers are more than willing to take the Father's place. They know right from wrong. And they will do right with a vengeance. And so all our wars are to make wrongs right. Reconciliation cannot be. First there must be justice. Hate is kindled, so wrong can be made right. And sometimes these elder brothers who will not be reconciled wear the garb of religion. These people will not be reconciled; they must first do the justice of God. But we clergy have always been more liable to the sins of the elder brother. It is an occupational hazard.

Back to the nature of the Father: God will not force us. If some Christians try to pressure us, we may overlook their excessive zeal. It is well-intentioned. But God does not force anybody to come home from the far country or to go in and be reconciled with his brother. Making peace with God is always voluntary. No one can make us love God. No one can make us seek forgiveness. No one can require that we be reconciled with our brother. We have to want to. And until we want to, any forced move in that direction will be false.

The Loving Father Never Stopped Loving

Comb the story through. Turn every word carefully. Look into every thought. Probe and explore to the bottom of it. But what we have is constant. The father is loving, and he never stops loving. Here are some evidences of his unbroken love:

He never gave up on the prodigal. He is pictured as waiting, looking, longing for the boy to come home again. In our own time, popular singers have gotten this idea across to us again. Remember the song about the fellow who is coming home and wonders if he will be welcome? Then there is the tree with all the yellow ribbons on it. He is welcome. Why? Because the father never quit loving.

He did not require penance from the prodigal. In fact, he would not even listen to his penitent speech. The boy was not allowed to perform as a servant; rather, he was made into a son again. How can so much be forgiven so quickly? Love. This is the story not of the prodigal; that story is lived out a million times over. The uniqueness of the story is the unfailing love of the father in spite of the prodigal.

He would not celebrate the return of his younger son without including his older son. The circle was broken. A part of the family was estranged; all of the family was hurting. So out he went to the boy who pouted. Patiently, he prevailed upon the elder brother to be a brother. He tried to reason with the boy. He tried to beg the boy. He owned the special relationship he had with the boy, "Son, you are always with me, and all that is mine is yours" (Luke 15:31, RSV). He just would not give up on the older boy any more than he would give up on the younger. It was an unfailing love.

He would not give up on reconciliation. The point of the gospel is reconciliation. We were separated from God in Eden. Sin has driven a wedge between God and all of us. But God has never been content with that separation. Always He has struggled to penetrate us, communicate to us, reach over and find us. But cats have a hard time understanding people. People have a hard time understanding God. And the wayward life has its own attractions. But God never gives up. He is trying first to reconcile us to Him, then He wants to reconcile brother to brother. This is the mission and message of a Loving Father.

I find this hard to take in. Everything in this life is conditional. If you do this, I will do that. But if you don't, the deal is off. Everything changes unless you perform up to stated expectations. But God is not that way. He does not give up on His children. He continues to work with prodigals. He stays with elder brothers. He just will not quit on us. To tell the truth, it makes no sense. Some of us aren't worth that much love. We've given the Father nothing but a hard time for a long time. But for reasons that make no sense from a human point of view, God stays with us. He keeps on chasing us to love us and win us back to Himself. This is the way God is.

Where did I get this message? It seems too good to be true. It ought to be treated with skepticism if I had made it up. But I didn't make it up. I got it from Jesus. He is the One who came from heaven with a special word for us. We could not understand God. He was unknowable. Jesus took on the form of man to show and to tell us what God was like. Jesus did things that make no sense when viewed from a human perspective. He loved us enough to die for us. He gave Himself to great suffering to save us from ourselves and our stubborn ways. But all of the story has to be strained.

Remember Elsa and the way she must have a hard time understanding why Dot and I do what we do? Now let's bring that story forward. God has reached from His otherness into our humanity. He has done so with a Son who has bridged the chasm between divinity and humanity. We will never completely understand why and what He did. But He is the best word we have on the ways and the nature of God. Jesus is our best clue into the expectations God has of us.

Jesus is our answer to the question every thinking person has to ask: What is God like? Look to Jesus. He is a Loving Father. He never stops loving us. He never stops loving all of us prodigals. He never gives up on all of us elder brothers. God just keeps on waiting for us. He really wants prodigals to come home. See Him standing out there? Looking. Waiting. He really wants elder brothers to come into the party. See Him out there reasoning, persuading? Won't you come home to your Father? Come into the party. He's a Loving Father.

12
The Pharisee and the Tax Collector

Luke 18:9-14

Let me put before you a strange dilemma. Every Sunday when you go to church you can count on the preacher pressing you to take your religion more seriously. By all sorts of appeals he asks you to dedicate yourself anew to Christ, to follow Him more seriously, to give yourself to Christ more completely. This is what all good preachers are asking their people to do. To be more earnest about your faith is good? Right? Right!

Now the other side of the coin: some of the most overbearing, one-sided, totally biased people alive on this earth are people who are taking their religious very seriously. Ian Paisley is the firebrand leader of the Irish Protestants in Ulster. He is unforgiving and given to a small spirit. So questionable is his character that our own State Department would not give Rev. Paisley permission to come to this country in 1983.

A synonym for bullying orthodoxy comes out of the Islamic world. The Ayatollah Khomeini led a revolt in Iran. He is first and foremost a religious man. No one takes his religion more seriously than Khomeini does. But the result of his commitment to his faith is not peace and love, rather it has become blood and blame. Even other Muslims fear and try to avoid confrontation with Khomeini.

Paisley is the true believer. Khomeini is body and soul a Muslim. Jesus knew people who were made of the same stuff; His parody of the true believer was the Pharisee.

If you think about it, some of the bad people, even the worst people, have been the people who took their religion most seri-

ously. If that be so, then why does your preacher try to get you
to take your religion more seriously? If you were to become the
more committed to Christ, does it follow that you would then
be like the Paisleys, the Khomeinis, and the Pharisees? Or, put
another way, what went wrong with the well-intentioned religious commitment of these earnest people? That is what this
parable is about.

Most of the people around us have some kind of religious
commitment. Ask them. They will tell you they are Baptists or
Presbyterians or other denomination. In fact, religion has little
to do with the way they order their lives. The morality of the
community is the yardstick these people use when they decide
what they are going to do. And since the yardstick has been
getting shorter and shorter for the past decades, there is more
and more that has become permissible. Jesus would be at home
with us. He lived among such a people. And interestingly, "the
common people heard him gladly" (Mark 12:37, KJV).

But alongside the masses who were casually religious was a
minority who were earnestly religious. These people were the
party of the Pharisees. Nearly all our references to Pharisees are
negative. They are the "bad guys" of the New Testament. This
sermon will not change this estimate, but I hope I can temper
it with some understanding of who they were and what they
stood for in the Jewish community.

Some two hundred years before Jesus, Palestine was ruled by
a Syrian king named Antiochus Epiphanes. This man had no
respect for the religion of the Jews. He did all he could to
persuade the Jews to abandon their religion. In an act that was
unspeakably profane, Antiochus Epiphanes ordered his soldiers
to kill a pig on the high altar of the Temple. If we understand
the Jewish aversion to swine, we can have some idea of just how
irreverent, how intolerant, how insulting this act of Antiochus
Epiphanes was.

But when the ruler of the land was doing all he could to keep
the Jews from their ancient faith, there sprang up from among
the people a small set of the faithful. They came to be known

as Pharisees. These few, at great peril to themselves, vowed a vow. They would be true to the laws of Moses no matter what the cost. At that time, the Pharisees were heroic. They risked themselves for a high cause. Most of the populace caved in to the bullying king. A brave few stood fast. It would be around people like them that the nation would rally in better days, and the faith of the fathers would make a comeback. These brave ones were the first Pharisees.

Two hundred years passed. The sons of the Pharisees did not forget their heritage. At considerable inconvenience and for no small price, the Pharisee practiced his religion. He took it seriously. A Pharisee would not cheat on his wife. A Pharisee would not pad his expense account. A Pharisee would not work on Sunday. A Pharisee would pay all of his taxes. A Pharisee would work at rearing his children in the ways of God. A Pharisee would study his Bible. A Pharisee would give to the Temple a full tithe of all he earned. A Pharisee would not forget his prayers.

If all this be so, then what went wrong? Why do the Pharisee come off as bad people? Herein hangs a tale, a tale that is as applicable today as in the time of Jesus. The more serious we take our religion, the more liable we are to fall into trap of the Pharisee. I know that it is easy to publicly whip the Pharisees. They lived a long time ago. None of them are going to get angry if we give them bad press. But I don't want to take that route. Most of us don't have the stomach to live by the rigor and the discipline of the Pharisees. Further, I think there is a larger picture that needs to be painted. Rather than just picking at the text, let's try to get from it the sense. Let's think about moral and spiritual growth.

The Way God Rears His Children

The Bible is filled with laws and teachings. Moses gave us the Ten Commandments. Jesus spoke the Sermon on the Mount. The Book of Proverbs is filled with wise sayings. All of these make a compendium, a veritable source book for right living. So when someone says, "I try to live by the Bible," we understand the frame of reference they are using. I can honestly say, shortcomings not withstanding, that I try to order my life by the Bible.

But to say that we try to live by the Bible does not deal with the problem. What is the Bible trying to do with us? How is God working with us? And more to the point: How is God trying to rear His children? This is what I want to say in a way you can understand. Here is a little acrostic that may stick in your mind:

(Write on scratch paper these three words: *paganism, legalism,* and *grace.* Make these words in the form of stairsteps. *Paganism* will be at the bottom. *Legalism* in the middle. *Grace* will be at the top of the ascending stair of words.)

Paganism. Untamed, savage, primitive—these are the words that have been used to describe our original condition. Left in our first state, we would be "me-first" people. The veneer of culture and civilization would quickly fall away. We would be little more than educated savages. In fact, education may have

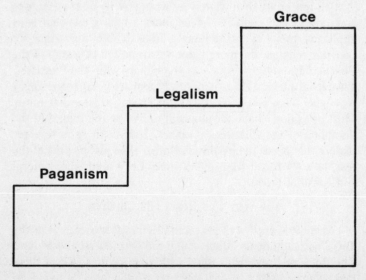

nothing to do with morality. Nazi Germany is a case in point. A very educated people performed gross sin. Karl Barth asked the question: "Which is a better mark for mankind, a good man on a horse or a bad man in an airplane?"

All of this has a theological dimension. In Genesis we are told that God put the human family out of the Garden of Eden. We had sinned. We had asserted ourselves against the rule of God. Pride, appetites, and temptation—each played its part. The human family had fallen. Whether in history we read of the harshness of the Spaniards in conquering the Aztecs, or whether in *The Lord of the Flies,* literature calls us to remember our fallenness, or whether a psychologist unravels the schemings of a self-willed person—all tell the old Bible story. We are pagan. We are fallen. And the good news in our Bible is that God is not content that we should stay in so depraved a state. God has moved to save us.

Legalism. God's great effort with the people of Israel was through Moses. Moses went into Egypt, found the slaves, and set about to gain their release. But it was not just into the wilderness these slaves went. They went to the sacred mountain. We know that mountain as Sinai. There God gave to the people a Law. The Law was long, and the Law was sealed with a covenant, but we call that Law the Ten Commandments. If the people were to do God's work in the world, they were to live by God's rules.

The rules were much more than just the Ten Commandments. How do you get your sins forgiven? How do you treat a neighbor who does you wrong? What do you do if you get sick? How do you treat your wife? How do you rear your children? What are you to do with the stranger who comes into your land? How do you worship? Who is to lead worship? On and on the list goes. We find these rules listed in the Old Testament. Moses said these rules were from God, and the people were to obey them. And though there was faith in the Old Testament, for the common people there was a set of rules. Do right, and one would be accepted of God.

The apostle Paul referred to the Law as "our schoolmaster" (Gal. 3:24-25, KJV). Here is the way *The Good News Bible* says it: "So the Law was in charge of us until Christ came, in order that we might then be put right with God through faith. Now that the time for faith is here, the Law is no longer in charge of us" (Gal. 3:24-25, GNB). Note that legalism is a step in the process. It is an upward step, but it is not the end of the process. God gave the Law just as God gave us grace. But the Law was not meant to be the end of the journey.

Grace. Finally, in the fullness of time, Jesus came. God had been leading His children toward grace all along. Grace is the reconciliation with God that has been needed since humanity's fall in Eden. It is through faith in Christ that God has changed us. We are no longer God's enemies; now we are God's friends (See 2 Cor. 5:18-19). The One we feared, we now want to be close to. The One we fled, we now run toward. The One we could scarcely take in is now at least understood in part thanks to the Word made flesh (See John 1:14). Because of grace we see God through the eyes of one who looks at Jesus.

There is a qualitative difference in legalism and grace. In legalism, *we must do our religion.* It is the doing that commends us to God. But in grace all is gift. God has given His own dear Son, the Good One for the bad ones. The apostle Paul put it this way: "When we were still helpless, Christ died for the wicked . . . It is a difficult thing for someone to die for a righteous person. . . . But God has shown us how much he loves us—it was while we were still sinners that Christ died for us!" (Rom. 5:6-8). This means that we did not earn our salvation. It is a gift. God has given it. In fact, Jesus is often described as God's gift (see John 3:16).

Though there is little change in the outward style of a legalist and one who lives under grace, the underlying presuppositions of legalism and grace are light-years apart. The one has earned his place with God. The other has been given place with God. The one is inclined to boast; the other knows that it is all a gift. God is trying to bring us out of paganism to legalism for a time.

But His real intention is to lift us on to grace. That is why Jesus came.

The Pitfalls of Child rearing

It's not easy to rear children. There are many pitfalls along the way. God is trying to bring us along, but we get tangled up in the growth process. In the first place, we do not get to move our children about in life as we would move the pieces on a chess board. They have a mind of their own. God has had the same problem. He has tried hard to move some of us. We have proven to have a mind of our own, a will so strong that we can even frustrate God's best wishes for us. But more than self-will, I want to line out a couple of risks in moral development:

The risk of making light of legalism. Preachers often make light of legalism. It is all bad. It is well below the New Testament. It is immoral to be legalistic. This is all partly true. The point is that legalism is a step above where most of the world is living. For some people life is a mess! It is a long row of cravings and appetites . . . appetites satisfied to the full. They are not legalists; they have always dreaded legalism. But for them legalism would order their lives. It would be a step up for them. Let's not condemn legalism out of hand. Every drug addict and alcoholic, every gambler and workaholic, every intemperate soul would be saved from much that is harmful if only they would come up to legalism. Let's be careful. Legalism is bad only when one is trapped in it. Getting to it is a salvation of a kind.

But some people have gotten to legalism. They have gotten there with a bang. It has been a big deal for them. Maybe it is a little like running for me. I needed to run. I was helped by running. And I have been insufferable in telling all about my running. For me, it was the hope of the world.

Compared to the moral earnestness of most of the people who were around Jesus, the Pharisees were truly orderly, disciplined, God-haunted people. They were the Puritans of their time. Anyone who knows Colonial history knows just how miserable the Puritans made everyone else with their religion. Puritans were right. They would order the land to their perception of God's way. Puritans could use the laws of the state to make people be good. (This idea is still with us.) Of course, Puritans were judgmental, severe, poor models of forgiveness and grace.

Pharisee behavior sometimes appears in earnest church people. We are taking our religion seriously. We are earnest, moral, straight. But we are hard to be around. We make others uncomfortable; they suspect that we judge them. Our prayers are not so much offered to God as they are testimonials to our own moral rectitude. One cynic said of a preacher's prayer that it was "the most eloquent prayer ever offered to a Boston audience."[1] Of course, the flaw here is that prayers are not to be offered to audiences but to God. And it is right here that the text bites. The Pharisee's prayer commended himself to God; his virtues were recited. And, finally, he put it all on the line: "I thank you that I am not like that tax collector over there" (Luke 18:11). This man's moral yardstick was his neighbor. Such are the sins of legalism when made the final point in the moral journey.

The Rules to Keep Us Straight

All the stories of Jesus point to rules to guide us. Three of these rules are in this story. If these rules are honored, they will keep us on track and keep us from getting trapped in legalism for a lifetime.

Pride destroys our perception. For all of the Pharisee's dedication, the Pharisee became a tragic figure. He kept the rules for so long until he came to think he had commended himself to God. God had not given him salvation; he had earned it. So the Pharisee's prayer was filled with a glowing estimate of himself. "I thank you God, that I am not greedy, dishonest, or an adulterer, like everybody else" (18:11). But keeping external rules does not amend our inward state, and sin is a matter of the heart.

I recall the time at the fat stock show in Fort Worth when I first stood in front of a mirror that made me look ten feet tall and six inches wide. It was some distortion of my real appearance! Pride makes us to think more of ourselves than we ought. Pride makes worship impossible. We do not need God; we are god!

An awareness of sin makes worship possible. The tax collector had no illusions about his moral condition. Whatever others thought of him, he knew he was sinful. This sure knowledge of need was the precondition that made forgiveness and God's grace possible. So while the rules-keeping man came to the Temple to tell God of his goodness, the sinner came to worship with no thought other than God. "God, have pity on me, a sinner!" is a good posture to begin any worship service (18:13). This is the frame of mind that opens the door to reconciliation.

God is the ultimate moral yardstick. This rule is crucial. If we go to church comparing ourselves to everyone else in the house, we have surely set in motion self-justification. Sometimes churchgoers with a twinkle in their eyes have gone out the back door saying, "He surely told 'em today." They are aware of what they are saying. They know that any word from God was not meant for "them;" it was meant for us, all of us.

I could make myself to look big if I should call a much shorter man to stand beside me. But that comparison would not last long. If another, taller man stood beside me, I would be the dwarfed one. Such is equally true in the moral arena. One is good only when compared to certain others.

William Barclay, in commenting on this story, told of an incident that happened on one of his journeys. He took the train from Glasgow to London. While riding south across the Yorkshire moors his eye fell upon a lovely, whitewashed cottage. It was shining brightly in the sun and looked so clean and white. A few days later he was on his homeward journey. A lovely snow had fallen. Soon the white cottage came into view. But in contrast to the snow, the clean cottage looked "drab and soiled and almost grey—in comparison with the virgin whiteness of the driven snow."[2] In much the same way, the Pharisee compared himself to the tax collector; the tax collector compared himself to the living God. All of us fall short when we measure ourselves by the words and life of Jesus. Jesus is our best insight into the holiness of God.

Moral progression is what God is about. He wants to save us from paganism. To do this He leads us into legalism. But legalism is not the end of the journey. In fact, if we stop there, we have aborted God's intention. It is the Pharisee's sin that he stopped short of what God had in mind for him. Go on. Move on up. God has sent His son, and all who give themselves into His care are given grace. This is where God has been leading us all along. Move on up. Step up to grace. It is amazing but true: the last step is not earned; it is for those who can accept the gift.

13
The Parable of Rejection

Luke 20:9-18

The game of cat and mouse is a part of every coached football game. The offense tries to corner and overcome the defense; the defense tries to stymie and frustrate the offense. But games of cat and mouse are not limited to sport. I have seen dialogue between husband and wife descend to cat-and-mouse games. "Whatever she wants, I am against." "If it was his idea, I am not going to do it." Such cat-and-mouse games can finally destroy the relationship.

There is cat-and-mouse game in the story of Jesus. When He was a boy, He was unknown and therefore unnoticed. When He was a young preacher, He was thought to have been of no consequence, just a spin-off of the ministry of John the Baptist. As He grew in popularity, the religious establishment had to take note of Him because the crowds were so drawn to Him. Finally, that same religious establishment decided Jesus could not be tamed or bought. He would have to be put down. He did matter, and He would not go away. Something had to be done. So the cat-and-mouse game began.

The porches of the Temple were a congregating place. Sometimes the talk was idle. But Jesus saw the milling, idle people as a field to be harvested. He never backed away from a chance to teach. So in an open, informal setting Jesus began to teach. Rather than let Jesus teach uninterruptedly, the "chief priests and the teachers of Law, together with the elders" (v. 1) bothered him with a question. These people did not want to learn anything from Jesus; they wanted to discredit him in front of a crowd. It was a game of cat and mouse. So they asked, "Tell us, what right do you have to do these things? Who gave you such right?" (Luke 20:2). What the religious leadership referred to were the miracles and the teachings of Jesus. If Jesus said He did what He was doing on His own authority, that was not enough. Who was He? Jesus was only a simple carpenter's son from Nazareth. If Jesus said He did what He did by God's authority, such would be called blasphemous. It was a no-win question for Jesus.

But that was not the end of the game. Jesus countered with a question: "Now let me ask you a question. Tell me, did John's right to baptize come from God or from man?" (20:3-4). Now Jesus had put His opponents in a tight place. If they said from God, Jesus would ask why the religious leadership did not honor John. If they said from man, the crowd surrounding them would rise up, for the crowd believed in John the Baptizer. The tables were turned.

How long could this cat-and-mouse game go on? Jesus had not come to play games; His mission was much more serious. To preach the nearness of the kingdom of God, to tell people there was hope, to act out forgiveness and grace—these were the principle parts of His mission.

The very next paragraph in Luke is a parable about rejection. In the first instance, the parable surely was aimed at His opponents in the game of cat and mouse. No doubt Jesus was referring to Jewish leadership and what they had done with the special mission of chosenness. The chance was wasted. God could not work through an ingrown, petty system. Even God could not communicate with them. They were the blind trying to lead the blind. If God were to speak to fallen humanity, He would need another voice. So Jesus came; the church was born.

In briefest fashion, I have outlined the sense of the parable and what it meant to the people to whom it was spoken. If I were to leave the matter here I would have addressed no more than ancient history. But it seems to me there is more here. Some truth is aimed, local, caught in time, and spoken to a particular situation. Other truth is larger. It has an application that is broad and timeless. Out of these larger truths we catch a glimpse of the ways of God with all people. The parable of the tenants in the vineyard is alive with timeless teachings.

Every Reasonable Opportunity

Like so many of the stories of Jesus, the setting is familiar. An owner, master, a landlord "planted a vineyard, rented it out to tenants, and then left home for a long time" (Luke 20:9). Suppose we see this parable this way: God made the world and put us in it to care for it. We are His stewards in the broadest sense. All of our lives are given over to keeping God's vineyard.

After a few years grapes come of the young vines. After a few years people grow up and become responsible. At this point the plot thickens. The owner sent a slave to get from his caretakers the rent to which he was entitled. The slave was beaten and sent back home with nothing. At this point the owner had a choice: he could go and punish and dispossess his unruly tenants or he could take a gentle and persuasive approach. He opted for the latter and sent a more important slave to collect the rent. This slave was handled roughly too. Again the option: Will it be harshness or will it be kindness? A third representative was sent. This representative was clearly recognized as an agent of the owner; he had rank. But this rank had no meaning to the caretakers. He was hurt; they threw him out. He went home with nothing.

By this time the owner would have been justified by custom to deal with his caretakers severely. They deserved it. Custom would have supported court action, eviction, and prosecution, conviction. But even at this extreme, the nature of the owner surfaced in a most peculiar way. His mind was different from other landlords. This unusual Owner reasoned with Himself: "What shall I do? I will send my own dear son; surely they will respect him!" (Luke 20:13). Here is a parable that acts out the opening lines of the Epistle to the Hebrews. "In the past God spoke to our ancestors many times and in many ways through the prophets, but in these last days he has spoken to us through his Son" (Heb. 1:1).

When you think about it, it makes no sense. The first servant, the second, and then the third—all were beaten, put out of the vineyard, and sent home with nothing. By what standard do we measure this owner? B. S. Easton said, "No man able to command force would risk a beloved son among such ruffians."[1]

Sometimes I hear a wit argue that our religion is just a creation of our imagination. It is something we have dreamed, imagined. Such would be reasonable were it not for the Bible picture of the nature of God. God is not like us. God is better than we are. So all the old texts come to life. "But God has shown us how much he loves us—it was while we were still sinners that Christ died for us!" (Rom. 5:8). And Martin Luther's favorite verse comes to mind: "For God so loved the world, that he gave his only begotten Son, that whosoever believeth in him should not perish, but have everlasting life" (John 3:16, KJV).

Often I hear people question the gentleness and the kindness of God. They seem to suggest that God is harsh, anxious to judge, and has a quick whistle. If I understand the God we know in Christ, all of us are being given every reasonable opportunity. The patience of God is really beyond what we deserve. Rather than accusing the Scriptures of painting a false picture of God, is it not the modern accusers who are painting a false picture of Him? If Jesus told us the truth about God, God has given us in the prophets, in Christ, in Paul and the apostles, in the church, in the Scriptures, in godly parents, in the witness of Christian friends, and in the countless chances all of us have had every reasonable opportunity to acknowledge God, pay His rent, and do His work. This teaching is timeless and is straight out of the sweep of biblical truth.

Calculated, Premeditated Rejection

Let's step back in time. Imagine yourself standing on the porch of the Temple listening to Jesus as He verbally spars with the Jewish leadership. When this parable was first spoken, who do you think came to mind when Jesus told of the repeated efforts of the owner to collect his rent? Who were these servants who were sent time and again? If I had been a reasonably informed Jew, I would have remembered Elijah, Isaiah, Jeremiah, and, lately, I would have remembered John the Baptizer. These were the servants who faithfully carried the message and tried to collect the rent. All were treated cruelly. All were handled roughly.

Was this rough treatment given the servants an accident? Was it a slipup? Did anyone go away from the event and reason, *We made a mistake. If the owner sends another servant, we must be more kind to him. If we are asked to pay the rent again, we must do it.* No such reasoning is in the text. More important, this kind of reasoning is not in the Old Testament. Moses called the Hebrews "a stiffnecked people" (Ex. 32:9, KJV). Isaiah plead with the people saying, "Come now, and let us reason together, saith the Lord: though your sins be as scarlet, they shall be as white as snow; though they be red like crimson, they shall be as wool" (Isa. 1:18, KJV). But reasoning did not work. They did not want to reason. They did not want to repent. They did not want to acknowledge God and pay rent to Him. They did what they did because they were the way they were.

God who revealed Himself in Christ is loving. He is kind. He is long-suffering. He is patient and gentle. He wants to forgive and receive. The father figure in the parable of the prodigal son is the way God is.

But alongside the picture of a loving God there must also be placed the companion theme: God expects us to acknowledge Him. We have to pay the rent. We are called to account.

These two ideas are equally true. They have to travel together. One can't have the head of a coin without getting the tail. So to tell of the love of God and leave out the expectation of accountability is to misrepresent God.

If we have to account and pay the rent, how are we doing? Not very well. From the Hebrews to the present we want the privileges of the use of the land, but we do not want to acknowledge the Owner. Sometimes we are mean. Sometimes we are sly. But both ways, we are trying to evade the servants who try to collect. I think one of the deep-down reasons some moderns do not hurry to the Christian religion is the picture the Christian religion draws of us. In this parable we look pretty bad. "When the tenants saw him, they said to one another, 'This is the owner's son. Let's kill him, and his property will be ours!' So they threw him out of the vineyard and killed him" (Luke 20:14-15).

Take the populace as a whole: there is no real effort to pay God the rent due Him. Take the church as a whole: the story is but slightly improved. The Jews wanted the privileges of chosenness, but they wanted none of the obligations. If the church I serve is a picture of the whole, we are not much better. All of us want to go to heaven when we die. All of us want the assurances that we are among the redeemed. But who wants to pay the rent? Who is ready to do the basic work of spreading the kingdom of God? I listen to our youth. They have plans to do this and be that. Only infrequently do I hear anyone say, "Here am I; send me" (Isa. 6:8, KJV). All the way down to the most mundane chores, again and again we want someone else to pay the rent. So we want our children to turn out well. We are anxious that they choose the Lord's part, but the basic rent of standing before those children as God's people—this basic rent is not paid.

What does the parable say? Unbroken, steadily, in calculated fashion, so many reject Christ and His ways. It is a calculated, premeditated rejection.

Reluctant, Final Judgment

When Jesus neared the end of the parable He began to speak of judgment. Here is the way He put it: "What, then, will the owner of the vineyard do to the tenants? . . . He will come and kill those men, and turn the vineyard over to other tenants" (Luke 20:15-16). I can hear the gasp from the crowd. It is written into the text. With one voice they said, "Surely not!" (Luke 20:16).

Let's give those people credit. They were obstinate, calculating, and cruel, but they knew what Jesus meant when He spoke the parable. They knew He was speaking of them. They knew He was speaking of undoing the covenant made with their fathers at Sinai. They knew He was speaking of judgment for Jews. They knew Jesus was saying that time had run out for Jewish reform; now God would find some other way to do His work in the world. The old tenants were to be replaced; new ones would be found.

Seems to me we are one with the Jews of old. When Jesus spoke of severe judgment, the crowd with one voice said, "Surely not!" When Jesus told of judgment in Matthew 25, the people who were condemned said, "When, Lord, did we ever see you hungry or thirsty or a stranger or naked or sick or in prison, and we would not help you?" (Matt. 25:44). Judgment never makes sense. Always there is time for one more chance. Surely, we deserve one more chance. Like Lot's wife, we look back longingly to our old ways. They were not so bad. Probably, there were people who were worse. Why should we be singled out for judgment? (Gen. 19:26).

Voltaire was a cynical fellow. He encouraged sin with a deft word. Often he would see a simple soul bound by teachings of childhood, and that man would delay over doing wrong. Voltaire would tease him as he egged him on saying, "God will forgive; it is His business." Such cartooning of God paints Him as an indulgent father, a Santa Claus who gives and gives and gives. To put God in your mind as forgiving is part of the truth. God is forgiving to all who take sin seriously, but opportunity long abused becomes its own judgment. Finally, God's patience runs out. We are called to account.

In what way does the parable continue to teach us? Let's make a modern parable of the old one. God is the owner; we are the tenants. We have been given great freedom in the way we manage God's world. But grapes do mature. Sometimes there is going to be a call to pay the rent. The servants have come. The Bible is ever before us. It is a powerful servant to call us to pay our rents. The church is less than perfect, but the church is the arena where the Spirit of God works. Out of the church comes a call to pay the rent. But the timeless quality in the story is as lively today as it was when Jesus first spoke. He tells us of the mind of God. "I will send my own dear son; surely they will respect him!" (Luke 20:13).

So through the broken vision of my writing, you have been told of the coming of the Son of God. He loves you. His coming postpones judgment. He has loved us even to the point of risking His life on our behalf. Since the Son has come, will you acknowledge Him, pay the rent? The Jews had a hard time recognizing Jesus for who He was. We are less trapped than were they. Sometimes the church stands in the way. Certainly, the world is ever blinding us to who He is and what He came to do. It is the deep desire of my heart that you see.

Can you see Him? He is Jesus; God's own dear Son. There is no judgment for all who recognize Jesus and cling to Him. In the Cross we escaped the worst of judgment. He took our sin upon Himself. But after Calvary we still must own Him, receive Him, and believe Him. The point of the parable of rejection is that we should not reject Him. Has the parable done its work in us?

Notes

Chapter One

1. *The Life and Times of Jesus the Messiah* (Grand Rapids, Mich.: William B. Eerdmans Publishing Co., 1971), p. 580.

Chapter Two

1. Walter Russell Bowie, *The Compassionate Christ* (Nashville: Abingdon Press, 1965), p. 152.
2. *Cambridge Greek New Testament for Schools and Colleges, St. Luke* (London: C. J. Clay and Sons, Cambridge University Press, n.d.), p. 254.
3. Ibid., p. 255.
4. Bowie, *The Compassionate Christ,* p. 151.
5. *Cambridge Greek New Testament,* p. 256.

Chapter Three

1. *Cambridge Greek New Testament for Schools and Colleges, St. Luke* (London: C. J. Clay and Sons, Cambridge University Press, n. d.),
2. William Barclay, *The Gospel of Luke* (Philadelphia: Westminster Press, n.d.), p. 168.

Chapter Four

1. John Keats, "When I Have Fears That I May Cease to Be," *British Poetry and Prose,* Vol. 2 (Boston: Houghton Mifflin Co., 1938), p. 209.
2. George A. Buttrick, ed., *The Interpreter's Bible,* vol. 8, (New York: Abingdon Press, 1952), p. 233.

3. H. J. Cadbury, *Jesus: What Manner of Man* (New York: The Macmillan Co., 1947), p. 45

Chapter Five

1. William Barclay, *The Gospel of Luke* (Philadelphia: Westminister Press, n.d.), p. 179.

Chapter Six

1. William Barclay, *The Gospel of Luke* (Philadelphia: Westminster Press, n.d.), p. 196.

Chapter Seven

1. *Cambridge Greek New Testament for Schools and Colleges, St. Luke* (London: C. J. Clay and Sons, Cambridge University Press, n.d.), p. 298-299.

Chapter Eight

1. George A. Buttrick, ed., *The Interpreter's Bible,* vol. 8, (New York: Abingdon Press, 1952), p. 265.
2. William Barclay, *The Gospel of Luke* (Philadelphia: Westminster Press, n.d.), p. 207.

Chapter Nine

1. *Cambridge Greek New Testament for Schools and Colleges, St. Luke* (London: C. J. Clay and Sons, Cambridge University Press, n.d.), p. 306.
2. William Barclay, *The Gospel of Luke* (Philadelphia: Westminster Press, n.d.), p. 212.
3. Walter Russell Bowie, *The Compassionate Christ* (Nashville: Abingdon Press, 1965), p. 209.

Chapter Ten

1. George A. Buttrick, ed., *The Interpreter's Bible,* vol. 8, (New York: Abingdon Press, 1952), p. 279.
2. *Cambridge Greek New Testament for Schools and Colleges, St. Luke* (London: C. J. Clay and Sons, Cambridge University Press, n.d.), p. 309.
3. Ibid., p. 310.

Chapter Twelve

1. William Barclay, *The Gospel of Luke* (Philadelphia: Westminster Press, n.d.), p. 232.
2. Ibid., p. 234.

Chapter Thirteen

1. B. S. Easton, *The Gospel According to St. Luke* (New York: Charles Scribner's Sons, 1929), p. 293.